The Mystical Glory of Sabbath

Matityahu Glazerson

Published by Kings Judaica, 2024.

THE MYSTICAL GLORY OF SABBATH

First edition. May 19, 2024.

ISBN: 979-8224076482

Written by Matityahu Glazerson.

*

The
Mystical Glory
of
SABBATH

*

Enlarged Edition

MATITYAHU GLAZERSON

****

The
Mystical Glory
of
SABBATH

****

Foreword
by Rabbi J. Salzer

Rabbi Matityahu Glazerson of the Torath Emeth Yeshiva, in Johannesburg, has rendered a great service to the Jewish public with the publication of his book.

It gives the English reader the opportunity to delve into connotations and layers of meaning in words and letters of the Hebrew language.

Rabbi Matityahu Glazerson disproves the notion that it makes no difference in which language you happen to read the Bible. He demonstrates that the Hebrew language possesses certain unique characteristics: a simple word expresses, in fact, deep ideas included within the literal meaning of the word.

The Torah is not reading material for leisure. Much effort is needed in order for one to be able to penetrate its real meaning and discover the deep beauty beneath the surface.

This book which Rabbi Glazerson presents to us is very timely, when thousands are searching for real values in a world of vanity.

Rabbi Glazerson teaches us to reach out for the eternal values which are to be found in our world when things are looked at from a proper perspective.

J. Salzer
Adath Yeshurun Congregation
Johannesburg
South Africa

Introduction

There is a vast wealth of tapped and untapped knowledge about the Jewish festivals and holy days. It is my hope that the reader, through the ensuing analysis of these momentous spiritual events, will appreciate his unique privileges and obligations as a Jew, and be encouraged to treat each of these, and other Jewish experiences, with proper, careful attention.

The true significance of our religious institutions is often masked by our indifferent, habitual attitudes. By using linguistic and numerological methods, we can break through this barrier of laissez-faire acceptance and discover the hidden meanings which lie at the core of the Torah's commandments.

Without utilizing these tools, we are as a man who stand outside a museum, content with observing the outer structure of the building, unaware of the beauties within.

My thanks to Mr. Seth Sprecher, for his translation of this book, and to all those involved in its writing, editing, and printing. To Shlomo Fox Ashrey the Translator of my book The Hidden Light of the Sabbath

The author

Matitahahu Glazerson

From the Secrets of the Holy Tongue

Foreword
On the Unique Status of Hebrew, the Holy Tongue
(From **Sefer HaPardess**, Chapter 1, **Shaar Ha-Otiot**)

Many have supposed that the letters of the Hebrew alphabet are a matter of symbolic convention. That is, the Sages decided and agreed among themselves that certain signs would represent the sounds of speech. For example, they agreed that the sounds made by closing the lips would be represented by the forms of the letters, **beit** (ב), **vav** (ו), **mem** (ם), and **peh** (פ) -- and likewise for the remaining sounds of the language. In the same way, other peoples also have symbolic representations for the sounds of their languages. According to this view, there is no difference between the Hebrew letters and the alphabets of other nations. The Hebrew letters are the conventional symbols used by the Israelite nation on the advice of Moshe through his prophetic inspiration, and the other alphabets are the conventional symbols of the other nations.

It follows, according to this theory, that the written words are nothing more than a means for making known the intent of the speaker. It is like a doctor who writes a book about the healing art. He doesn't intend that the book itself will be medicine. Rather, he intends that the book should make known his thoughts or preferences on the subject of healing. Once the reader understands the principles of the healing art as written in the book, the book itself is of no importance whatever. Thus, if a person studies the book for years on end but does not succeed in learning the principles set forth therein, his study has done nothing for him and his soul has not been improved at all, since he still does not understand the requirements of the art. In fact, his study has actually done him harm, since he has wasted time and effort without gaining understanding.

The Torah, according to those who hold this view, is just like the medical textbook of our example. The purpose of the Torah is to reveal the inner meanings and processes necessary for the perfection of the soul. Thus, if one does not master the required knowledge, he gains no benefit from his studies — G–d forbid.

This theory cannot be true, for undoubtedly the words of Torah "restore the soul" (**Psalms** 19:8). The proof is that the **halachah** obligates us to read the weekly Torah portion, "twice in the original Hebrew and once in the Aramaic translation," and this includes even seemingly meaningless place names such as "Atarot and Divon" (**Numbers** 32:3). This teaches us that the Torah is perfect. The words and letters themselves have hidden inner meaning, spiritual power, and vitality.

GUIDELINES TO GEMATRIA

(adapted and abridged from material prepared by Rabbi Shlomo Fuchs)

Throughout our **Haggadah**, we have analyzed Hebrew words in terms of their numerical value, arrangement of letters and so on. This system is called **gematria**, and it will be useful to summarize some of its basic principles before embarking on our commentary.

"Primary Gematria"

The thirty-two principles of exegesis used by **Chazal** to interpret the Torah are set forth in a **braitta** in the name of Rabbi Eliezer, the son of Rabbi Yossi HaGelili. The twenty-ninth principle is that of "primary **gematria**", a system whereby the numerical value of each letter of a word is counted, and then totalled. The commentary **Midrash Tannaim** states that the numerical values of the Hebrew letters were given to Israel at Mt. Sinai. Their values are as follows:

1 – א	10 – י	100 – ק
2 – ב	20 – כ	200 – ר
3 – ג	30 – ל	300 – ש
4 – ד	40 – מ	400 – ת
5 – ה	50 – נ	500 – ך
6 – ו	60 – ס	600 – ם
7 – ז	70 – ע	700 – ן
8 – ח	80 – פ	800 – ף
9 – ט	90 – צ	900 – ץ

Thus, the "primary gematria" of פרנסה (parnassah, "livelihoood")
is 395: 80+200+50+60+5 = 395.

"Reduced Gematria" or "Small Numerical Value" ("Mispar Katan")

The **Mispar Katan** is the "primary gematria" with any final
zeroes removed. Thus, 10 or 100 are both counted as 1. Sometimes the
"primary **gematria**" or "**mispar katan**" is reduced even further by
adding together all the digits of the number. For example, we saw
above that the **gematria** of פרנסה is 395. This can ultimately be
reduced to 8: 3+9+5 = 17; 1+7 = 8.

"Full Gematria"

In this form of **gematria**, each letter of a word is written out in
full, and the numerical value of all the resulting letters is counted. For
example, the "full **gematria**" of the word קר (kar, "cold") is calculated
in this manner: קוף ריש – 100+10+80; 200+10+300 = 696.

Interchangeability of Letters Which Are Formed in the
Same Part of the Mouth

Sefer HaYetzirah, an ancient kabbalistic work, states that the
letters may be divided into five groups, based on the part of the mouth
where the letter is produced.

1. אחה"ע: These are the gutteral letters formed in the
   throat, using the back of the tongue and/or the pharynx.

2. בומ"פ: These are the labial letters, formed primarily by
   closing the lips.

3. גכ"ק: These are the palatal letters, formed mainly by
   contact between the palate and the back third of the
   tongue.

4. דטלנ"ת: These letters are produced with the tip of the
   tongue against the front of the palate just behind the
   teeth.

5.   דסשר״צ: These are the sibilants, produced by expelling air between the teeth with the tongue held flat.

The Addition of the Kollel

Sometimes, in finding the numerical equivalent of a word, we increase the total by one. Rabbi Y.A. Chaver, in **Pitchei Shearim** (p. 252), explains that in such cases the root of a word is still attached to the upper world.

A related practice in **gematria** is to find the total numerical value of a word, and then to add the number of letters of that word. By this method, the word רגל (**regel**, "foot"), has a numerical value of 236: 200+3+30+3 (the number of letters of the word).

The **Baal Ha'Turim** finds a Scriptural basis for the practice of adding the **kollel** to a **gematria** in the verse "Efraim and Menashe will be the same as Reuven and Shimon . . . " (**Genesis** 48:5). When combined, the names "Efraim" and Menashe" have a numerical value of 726, while "Shimon, Reuven" have one of 725. Thus, when we add the **kollel** to the second pair of names, the values of both pairs are equal. And, as explained above, the Torah itself testifies that Efraim and Menashe, and Reuven and Shimon "will be the same."

אפרים, מנשה (Efraim, Menashe):
1+80+200+10+40+40+50+300+5 = 726
ראובן, שמעון (Reuven, Shimon):
200+1+6+2+50+300+40+70+6+50 = 725
1 (the **kollel**) + 725 =   726

***

As taught by **Chazal**, one cannot use **gematria** to introduce Torah innovations which are not confirmed by our early forefathers who had direct and trustworthy traditions. However, one may use **gematria** to uphold the teachings of our Sages and the traditions of our forefathers, and whoever originates such **gematriot** – more power to him, and his reward will be great. For this purpose, the scholar is allowed to search tirelessly for a **gematria** with which to support the words of truth.

The Sabbath

The Uniqueness of Sabbath

The connotation of the word "Sabbath", שבת, when explained according to its simplest meaning of "rest," is only a small part of the full significance of the word.

Rabbi Samson Raphael Hirsch, in his exposition of the Torah, says, that the word Sabbath, indicates the cessation of, an activity in progress.

The idea is expressed by our honored sages, in Mechilta (an exposition of the book Exodus) where the passage, "Six days thou shalt do all thy work" is explained to mean, that one should rest as if his work was completed.

An additional explanation is, that one should rest from even the thought of work, and that man is obligated on the Sabbath, not only to rest from labor and creative activity, but also to separate him from them totally.

He must lock his work out; remove it completely from his thoughts. This corresponds to the removal of חמץ (leaven) at Passover. פסח symbolizes the power of man, which is bound up with the creative powers of God.

On Passover it is incumbent upon a person to neutralize his strength, to surrender his pride. For this reason, Passover is also known as "Shabbath," as the Torah states, "And you shall count for yourselves, from the day following the Shabbath."

According to the theory, expounded by Rav Saadiah Gaon, and others, the first two letters in the root of a three-letter Hebrew word, are the essence of the word, discontinuation, and severance as in, for example, the words שבר (to break or disconnect) and שבב (piece).

This applies to many other words, as Rabbi Munk says, and therefore expresses its primary significance. Accordingly, word roots that begin with שׁב, indicate expressions of states, at the end of his book, The Seven Days of Creation.

Therefore, on the Shabbath, a man is required to cut himself off completely, from the ordinary secular weekdays, something which cannot be attained by mere physical rest, but rather requires spiritual effort, with the aid of the sanctity of the Shabbath.

THE MEANING OF THE WORD שבת

Another meaning of the word שבת ceasing indicates to what the holy Zohr says that on Shabbath the forces of evil cease their activities, and do no harm to mankind, and thus the shabbath protects the Jew from the impurity of sin.

The theory that the main letters in all Hebrew word-roots, are the first two letters, and that the third letter represents an additional aspect, can be understood through that which I wrote in my book, "Letters of Fire".

This book suggests that each letter has a special significance, which we can learn from our sages in many different places, and in particular from the book, "The Letters of Rabbi Akiva."

The last letter in a word-root, gives the meaning of the word since it is the object of the activity, indicated by the first two letters of the root.

In the light of this explanation, it is possible to say that the word שבת, indicates to the breaking off (שב) of the ת, the letter which according to The Letters of Rabbi Akiva, symbolizes lust and desire.

The letter ת itself, is called תאו, from the word תאוה, which means lust. Thus, on the Shabbath, a man is obligated to totally disassociate himself from lust and desire, and curtail his materialistic activities.

The word שבת, also has a positive significance, according to Rabbi Samson Raphael Hirsch, since it is close in pronunciation, to the word שפט (to judge), this similarity, is meant to teach us that just as the verb שפט, means essentially the designating of everything to its proper place in the world, so too in שבת, lies the power to ascribe to man and the world their proper place.

The atmosphere of the Shabbath, inspires man with broad knowledge, through which he is able to recognize in proper perspective his place, and task, in the world.

The positive and negative implications of the word Shabbath, are inextricably bound, for a man can his proper place, only if he removes himself from his normal everyday activities, and the lustful nature of materialism.

THE LETTERS שב ARE THE BASIS OF THE שבת

This is because he cannot reach valid conclusions concerning his duty in this world, while his mind and knowledge are occupied with materialistic work.

According to the explanation, that the first two letters of the root are the essence of the word, we can relate the word שבת, to the word שבץ (to set, arrange), in that the Shabbath, can arrange everything in its prescribed boundary, and appropriate place.

A deeper explanation, through mysticism, of the connection between the word שבת and the word שבץ, can be understood from our mystical books.

In them, it is written, that the quality of the Shabbath, is that of glory.

This is the quality of Jacob, our father, about whom the sages say, "One, who keeps the Shabbath according to its regulations, merits the unlimited inheritance, just as Jacob our father, merited."

Rashi explains that Jacob kept the Shabbath, as it is written, "And he encamped before the city."

Our sages tell us that the word "encamped", means that he established the boundaries of the city, for the purpose of Techum Shabbath (a boundary limiting walking distance on Shabbath).

Each letter in the root the word פאר (glory), precedes one of the letters in the root of the word שבץ (to set), in the order of the alphabet (פ before ץ, א before ב, and ר, before ש).

This teaches us, that the quality of glory is the vehicle through which all things are arranged in total harmony, as is generally known.

The characteristic of glory is the balance between loving-kindness. Which, mystically speaking, is on the right, and might, which is on the left.

Each letter of the word שבת, follows one of the letters of the word ראש (head, beginning, prime), in the order of the alphabet, and this alludes to the lofty source of the Shabbath, as Rabbi Jacob Emden comments, in his book "Beith Yaakow", on the verse, "מראש מקדם נסוכה" ("From the beginning ,it was ordained") in the Shabbath: song, Lechah Dodi.

THE THREE MEALS OF THE SABBATH

According to our holy books, the three meals that are eaten on the Shabbath, correspond to the supreme attributes. The most sublime one of these meals, being the Saturday morning, one which corresponds to עתיקא קדישא (the Ancient Holy One).

The word עתק (ancient), the root of עתיקא, connotes a supernal realm which is completely removed from our world.

The supreme loftiness of this upper world, is revealed in the letters of the word עתק, which precede the letters פאר (glory, praise), in the order of the alphabet. Shabbath obtains its sanctity, from these upper worlds of antiquity and glory.

The words ראש and פאר both contain the letters אר, (light), which allude to the ethereal illuminations, hidden in these worlds.

The spiritual light comes to us, dressed in the form of the Shabbath, as is reflected by the first two letters of the word שבת, שב, and the letters which follow אר (light) in the order of the alphabet.

The Shabbath, in its essence, is God's light which fills man, and the entire world.

The powerful light of the Shabbath, penetrates even through the ordinary layman of Israel, thus, as our sages tell us, an ordinary layman who is suspected on weekdays as to whether he has removed the tithe, is nevertheless trusted on the Shabbath, and he is believed if he says that he has already done it. The awesomeness of the Shabbath, is on this people, and they will not lie.

SABBATH FOUNDATION OF THE WORLD

The Shabbath is the foundation of the World to Come, and those who properly enjoy the Sabbath earn for themselves the experience of eternal life and total truth and purity.

On the Shabbath the soul attaches itself to the original source of eternal life from which it came.

The Sages of the Kabbalah teach that the, numerical value 400, the last letter of the alphabet, letter ת represents the World to Come.

For this reason, writes Rabbi Tzaddok HaKohen (Pri Tzaddik), when the Gemara deals with matters of this world it uses the number 300 and not 400.

The letter ש has the numerical value 300, indicating the three dimensions of this world, but the letter ת has the numerical value 400 and represents the four dimensions which are present in the World to Come.

According to the Sefer HaYetzirah, (The book of Creation, related to Abraham. our fore forefather Sabbath was created with the letter ת.

The Sabbath, the wellspring of the World to come, is created through the letter ת , the letter of the World to Come.

The return of the soul to its source in the World to Come is revealed through the construction of שבת from שב and ת.

The first part, which the word שב means "return." Thus, the letters שב –ת indicates the return of the soul to ת, the World to Come.

The soul returns to its source and clings to it, but all this is dependent upon the ability of man to abolishשב)) lust full instinct (. (ו,תאת

THE HEAVENLY SOURCE OF THE SABBATH

To recognize the heavenly origins of שבת (Shabbat), we have only to look at its numerical value, 702, or expressed differently, 700 + 2.

The number 700 represents the lofty source of the 7 days of creation, because as the Kabbalah tells us, the decimal system of hundreds, tens, and ones represents the upper worlds, the hundreds being higher worlds than the tens, and the tens being higher worlds than the ones.

Regarding the holy seventy-two-letter name of G-d, the Zohar (Ra'aya Mehemna, part 2, p. 92b) says that there are seventy main letters and the other two serve as witnesses.

The same can be said about now, that it is essentially the channel of emanations from the upper worlds (represented by 700) and the witnesses to this process (represented by 2).

The fire of the Sabbath devours the fires of pride, lust, and jealousy. Each of these characteristics is compared to fire in many texts, and it is explained that pride, lust, and jealousy are three negative forces which Abraham, Isaac, and Jacob fought against.

Abraham battled lust with his Chessed (Kindness) and devotion; Isaac combated pride, the root of idolatry, by offering himself unconditionally to G-d; and Jacob, the man of truth and peace, fought jealousy and bloodshed.

The pure, holy fire of the three Patriarchs which burns on the Sabbath consumes and nullifies the evil fires which oppose them and the harmful roots are laid to rest.

This is another property of the Sabbath revealed through the letters of שבת. The word נשבתים, (Nishbatim) means "laid to rest,"

THE AWE OF SABBATH

The fear of Heaven, even that of common laymen, is reinforced on Shabbath, because יראה (fear), in its fundamental origin is ראיה (vision), the vision of the reality of the Creator and Supervisor of the world.

An illustration of this is found in the Jerusalem Talmud (Demai, ch.4),where we learn that if an unlearned jew states that produce has btithed, we suspect him of lying and we cannot eat the food without tithing it. This applies if he made the statement on a weekday.

But if he stated on the Shabbath that produce had been tithed, we are permitted to believe him. We do not suspect him on lying then, because "the awe of the Shabbath is upon him."

The light of the Shabbath, illuminates the mind of man, enabling him to

The connection between the Shabbath, and fear is revealed by the first word of the Torah, בראשית, (in the beginning), for the Zohar explains, that it is a combination of the letters of the words יראה, and שבת, and that fear and Shabbath have been connected with one another, ever since the creation of the world.

The Shabbath, is the culmination of the act of Creation, as the verse states, "And God finished, on the seventh day".

On the seventh day, the last step of Creation, was completed, as King Solomon, the wisest of all men said, "The end of the matter, all having been heard, fear God, and keep His commandments, for this is the whole of man.

Even an unlearned jew will not lie on the Shabbath, due to the awe inspired by the special light of the shabbath. The word fear יראה appear at letter skip of two, in the phrase, And GOD blessed the seventh day"(Genesis 2:3)ויברך אלהים את יום השביעי

On this verse, the Midrash comments: "He blessed it with light." The connection between the Shabbath and the concept of awe is manifested in the first word of the Torah, בראשית - Bereishit, "In the beginning").

In different order its letters spell ירא שבת (yarei Shabbath, "in awe of the Sabbath"). Similarly, the holy Ari taught (Likutei Torah, siman 17) that the Shabbath is identified with the quality of awe, the quality of ירא שבת. The letters of בראשית (Bereishit, "In the beginning") in different order also spell ברית אש (brit esh, "covenant of fire"), a concept connected with the Sabbath, as we have seen above.

The numerical value of the word יראה awe is 216) is connected with the fire of the covenant or brit ברית , numerical value 612), and both of these are connected with the Sabbath. As it is known the foundation of woman is her awe of G-d. This is expressed in the passage Eshet Chayil, "A Woman of Valor" (Proverbs, ch. 31), which we recite on Sabbath night, concluding: "Charm is false and beauty is vain. A woman who is in awe of G-d, she shall be praised."

THE PURPOSE OF CREATION, FEAR OF GOD

Awe of G-d is the purpose of Creation. This can be seen in the word "Creation" (Bri'ah, בריאה), whose letters in different order spell ביראה (beyir'ah, "for the sake of awe") (Chiddushei HaRim to Genesis 1:1).

King Solomon, the wisest of all men teaches us in Ecclesiastes (3:14) that the purpose of Creation is so that man can achieve awe of G-d.

There he writes: "G-d created [everything) so that [mankind] should be in awe of Him." Again, he writes in the concluding the verse of Ecclesiastes says: "Be in awe of G-d and keep His commandments, for this is the whole [purpose] of man."

Some commentators point out that the word ("And...were completed..." in the passage "And the heavens.

The purpose of Creation was, to bring man to a fear of Heaven; "And God hath so made it, that man should fear before Him."

Also, within the materialistic cloak of the land, is preserved the spiritual light, as is seen by breaking up the word ארץ (land), into אר (the element of light) and ץ.

The purpose of the Creation is to awaken the respectful fear, spoken about above. This is revealed through the word בריאה (creation), which is a composite of the letter ב (symbolizing the word, בית or house) and יראה (fear).

As for יראה, Fear, it is cited in a commentary on the Torah, called Chidushei HaRim, that the whole purpose of Creation is to inspire this fear.

For us, the creations, the בריאה, is a ב (house) for יראה (fear).

In other words, an environment in which to learn fear of God.

On Shabbath, the housing and outer garment of this fear is removed and the inner core of the fear itself is revealed in full force.

According to the book of formation, the Torah itself commands us to be in awe of the Shabbath, for it is (Leviticus, 26:2)"Guard my Shabbath and be in awe of My Sanctuary.

In this verse, says the book HaYereim the phrase "be in awe", refers not only to the Sanctuary, but also to the Shabbath.

To elucidate the deeper meaning of the command, the Sages (Yevamot, 6a) "It is not the Shabbath of which you are in awe, rather you are in awe of Him Who commanded about Shabbath".That is our awe of the Shabath demonstrates our awe of the creator.

The Light ((אור)of the Shabbath arouses ((מעורר)in a person a feeling of embarrassment when he realizes how small and insignificant he is compared creator.(The linguistic root of light –אור is interchangeable with the root of "arouse", עור 'since the letter א and the letter ע are both pronounced at the back of the throat).

THE LIGHT ON THE SABBATH

About the Light of the Shabbath, states the holy Zohar, the lights of the three Patriachs, symbolized by the three branches of the letter ש, are united with the Jewish woman.

The holy Zohar explains it , as it is alluded to by the word שבת which can be analyzed, as , ש-בת where the letter ש stands for the three Patriarchs, and בת meaning "daughter" or "woman" refers to the Jewish woman, about whom we sing on Shbbath eve,

"A woman of valor who will find" (proverbs, 31). The light of the shabbath is the source of this day's restfulness.

Regarding the verse in Genesis (49:15)"And he saw rest, that is good". Maor Vashemesh writes "On all the ordinary days of the week, the light and holiness are clothed in many garments, and because of these garments' it is impossible to see the light of holiness.

But when the Holy Shabatth comes, it is as our Sages said "when the Holy Shabbath arrived, rest arrived".

Then the hidden light is revealed to the righteous, to each one according to his spiritual level.

THE NUMBER THREE AND THE SABBATH

The number Three represents the Three Patriarchs who are the foundation of the world' existence.

The Sages teach us in Pirkei Avot, (1:2):" The world stands on three things, on the Torah, on the service of GOD, and on the act of Kindness".

These three things are epitomized by the three Patriachs. Jacob epitomizes Torah, Isaac epitomizes service, Abraham epitomizes loving kindness.

At the end of the same chapter of Pirkey Avot, we find a similar dictum of the Sages: "The world exists by virtue of three things, Justice, Truth, and Peace".

These three things also are epitomized by the three Patriarchs: Isaac epitomizes Justice, Jacob Truth, and Abraham peace.

These number "three" (שלשה) is the foundation of the world.

This fact is encoded in the first verse of the Torah "In the beginning GOD created Heavens and Earth" .

(בראשית ברא א-ל-ה-י-ם את השמים ואת הארץ)

If we begin with the first letter ש in this verse, and take every seventh letter, we find the word "שלשה" -" three".

This teaches that the principle of the number three is built by means of the principle by seven, which corresponds to the Shabbath , the Seventh Day.

The idea of the three which complete seven, making a total of ten, is revealed in the holy Zohar (Part 3, p.273) "One must eat three meals on the Shabbath, for these complete the seven benedictions of the prayer, bringing them to the perfection of ten.

From this we see that the three meals of of the Shabbath are considered equal in importance to the seven benedictions of the Shabbath Prayers.

The word "seven" (, (שבע alludes to names of GOD- י-ה-ו-ה, which denotes the attribute of Mercy, and the name of GOD א-ל-ה-י-ם -, which denotes the attribute of Justice.

These two names are connected with the creation of the world ,as we find in the verse (Genesis2:4): "These are the generations of the heavens, and the earth ,on the day the lord, GOD made earth and heavens,",where the creator is referred to as the Lord GOD. י-ה-ו-ה- א-ל-ה-י-ם

The word שבע (seven) consist of two parts ש-בע each part referring to one of these two names of GOD.

The first part, the letter to the full numerical value א-ל-ה-י-ם while the second part the letters, בע refers to numerical value of the name of GOD, י-ה-ו-ה .

This is the numerical value of those names GOD:

א-אלף-111

ל-למד-74

ה-הי-15

י-יוד-20

ם-מם-80

Total -300

This is the numerical value of the letter ש

The numerical value of the name of GOD – י ה- ו -ה– -is as follows:

י-יוד -20

ה-הי- 10

ו-ויו-22

ה-הי-15

Total-72

This is the numerical value of the letters בע

From we glimpse the importance of the number seven –שבע as major underlying principle in the creation of the world.

בשת-SABBATH AND שבת - EMBARRASSMENT

Thus, the holy Zohar (Tikunei Zohar, tikun 6, p. 24a) says that the Sabbath involves the attribute of ירא בשת -Yere'reh, boshet, "be in awe, embarrassment"), which is spelled with the same letters as בראשית (Bereishit, "In the beginning...").

Likewise the holy Ari, the KabbalistRabbi Isaac Luria, pointed out that the same letters that spell שבת (Shabbath, also spell בשת (boshet, embarrassment"), alluding to the sense of embarrassment that the Jewish person feels on the Holy Shabbath.

The realization on the Shabbath that G-d is the Bestowed and the Emanating Source from whom we receive all the life-giving, spiritual and material abundance - it is this realization that causes us to feel embarrassed and humble.

"Light" (orah, אורה) brings a person to "embarrassment" (bushah, בושה), as seen in the letters ofבושה , which follow immediately after the letters ofאורה in the Hebrew alphabet.

These two words, have two letters in common, the letter ה and the letter ו.

The remaining two letters of בושה namely the letter ב , and the letter ש , follow immediately after the remaining two letters ofאורה .

The word בושה is spelled with the same letters as שובה , for בושה (bushah, "embarrassment") is the foundation of שובה (shuwah), meaning "return" or "repentance," as it is written (Hoshea 14:2): "Return (שובה) O Israel to the Lord your G-d."

The connection between the Shabbath and repentance can be seen in Midrash Yalkut Shimoni (1:38), which states:

Adam met Cain. He asked him: "What was the outcome of your trial? " He answered: 'I repented and stopped sinning."

Adam slapped himself on the cheek and said: "This is the power of repentance, and I did not know it? Immediately Adam arose and sang (Psalms 92): "A melody, a song for the Sabbath Day."

From this we see, that the essence of the Shabbath is to return to the Source; and returning to the Source is the root of repentance (teshuvah תשובה).

Awe of G-d (yir'ah, יראה), according to the Kabbalah, is connected with the sefirah of Malchut (Kingship), the seventh sefirah counting from Chessed (Kindness;).

The connection between awe (יראה) and the "seventh" is manifested in the verse, "And G-d blessed the seventh day" (יברך א-ל-הים את יום השביעי ויברך אותו) (Genesis,2:3).

Sabbath and Repentance

השבת (the Shabbath). has the exact same letters as the word תשבה (repentance), to teach us that the Shabbath, is the designated time for repentance for wayward actions done by man during the regular weekdays.

The atmosphere of the Shabbath, awakens in man, feelings of regret and repentance, for his bad deeds.

The first to come to repentance through the Divine inspiration of the Shabbath, was Adam.

About him, our sages say in a Midrash (the deeper explanations of the Torah) that with the entrance of the Shabbath, he repented for his sin, and sang, "A psalm, a song for the Shabbath day, It is good to give thanks to the Lord ...,".

In which he expressed the greatness of the Shabbath, and, particularly, its power to arouse in man admiration of God's works -thereby bringing him to confession of his evil deeds, and full repentance before God.

The Shabbath light, which brings man to repentance, is indicated by the letters שב of the word שבת, which follow the letters אר (light) in the order of the alphabet.

Man returns penitently to his Creator with the revelation of the Shabbath light.

The letters יראה (fear), precedes the letters שיבה (repentance), because the prime motivation for repentance, is when man truly recognizes, that there exists an Observer, of all his actions.

The relationship between יראה and שיבה, is revealed through the main letters of יראה (the אר) coming before the main letters of שיבה (the שב) in the order of the alphabet.

The letters שבת, are the same as those in the word בשת (shame, embarrassment), to show us that the principal prerequisite for the initiation of repentance, is the shame and embarrassment a man feels for his ugly deeds, because one who is ashamed of his sins, already stands on the path of repentance, as our sages say, "He who is ashamed of his sins is pardoned for his crimes."

The source of shame is fear of Heaven, for through this a man realizes that all of his actions are witnessed by the Creator of the world.

With the inspiration of the Shabbath light, a man comes to be ashamed of his deeds and returns penitently to his Creator.

The world exist by the merit of the Shabbath and all aspects of the Shabbath are double-for example the loaves bread-at each meal, the two lambs offer as the Shabbath Additional Offering and so on.

This is because the foundation of the sabbath is זכור -remember and שמור -guard.

Sabbath Defined Mathematically

The content of the Shabbath, is expressed by the illumination of God's Divine Light. This fact is evident, through the use of small numerical value, or minor numerology (only the single units of ones, tens and hundreds being used). The word, שבת, in minor numerology, is equivalent to 3 (9 = (ת) 4 + (ב) 2 + (ש.

And similarly, the word אור (light), in minor numerology, is equivalent to 1 (9 = (ר) 2 + (ו)6 + (א.

Another word which is numerically equivalent to אור number 9, in minor numerology is the word אמת (truth), 1 (9 = (ת)4 + (מ)4 + (א.

The equivalence in numerical values of שבת and אמת, comes to teach us that the awareness of truth, is more abundant on the Shabbath, is the time when a man is able to judge his actions truthfully and honestly.

The number 9 expresses truth and eternity, as Iben Ezra says about the verse "True language will stand for ever".

This is supported by the fact that when the number 9 is multiplied by any numeral, the digits of the sum always add up to 9.

For example: $9 \times 2 = 18$ (1 + 8 = 9), $9 \times 3 = 27$ (2 + 7 = 9), etc. All this, comes to teach us that pure truth, and clean light, are eternal, and the same is true for the Shabbath.

For this reason, the Shabbath, is called ברית עולם

(Everlasting Covenant). The word ברית (covenant) is also equivalent to 9, using minor numerology 2 (= (ת)4 + (י) 1 + (ר)2 + (ב 9.

Because it is an eternal covenant, שבת is closely identified with ברית, as verified by their equal numerical values.

The bond between שבת and ברית, is suggested by the first word of our Torah, בראשית, whose letters can be arranged to spell both ברית אש (covenant of fire), and ירא שבת (fear Shabbath).

The word ברית is equal in full numerology to 612, alluding to the 612 commandments of the Torah, aside from the commandment of ברית itself. The Shabbath, like ברית, is considered by our sages to be equal in importance, to the whole of the Torah.

The covenant ברית, refers also to theברית מילה , circumcision, which like the Shabbath are a sign of the unique status of the Jewish people.

This is reflected in the fact that the numerical value of the words ברית מילה "the covenant of Circumcision", is the same numerical value as the word 702 - שבת.

The Shabbath, as the day designated for repentance, is also suggested by the fact that the initial letters of the words שבת בו תשובה (in Shabbath there is repentance) spell שבת.

Repentance is dependent upon the Shabbath, since repentance is returning to the source and root of man's soul, and the Shabbath, as we have seen, is the concealed source and original shoot imploring man to reestablish the link with his soul's root.

The connection between the Shabbath, and the upper worlds, is revealed in the letters תגא (crown) which follow the letters שבת, in the order of the alphabet, the letter ת after the letter ש, the letter ג after the letter ב, and the letter א after the letter ת (restarting the alphabet).

This Aramaic word תגא, alludes to the upper world, the world of the crown, since, as, the Aramaic language also has holiness because it is known sense, a "garment" of the holy tongue Hebrew, and was used to translate it in the Targum.

Sabbath's Special Gift

A great gift of Shabbath is the quality of Knowledge (דעת), as it is said (Exodus 31:13)" Observe my Shabbath, for it is a sign between Me and you for your generations to know לדעת that I am GOD, who sanctify you".

Ben Ish Chai finds an allusion to this in the inner numerical of the full letters of the word שבת , Shabbath .

The inner numerical value of the full letters, is found by spelling out the names of the letters and then, dropping the first and outer letters, of each name.

The inner full letters שבת Shabbath,ש ין,ב ית ת ו ,the inner letters,ו ין-ית-י - - whose total numerical value is 476, which equals the numerical value of the , בדעת meaning ,with knowledge which the heart Jew on the

From knowledge and understanding stem Joy, which fills the heart of the Jew, who keeps the Shabbath. The connection between the heart and the Shabbath is revealed by spelling out the names of the letters of the heart, לב: למד בית.

The numerical value of the inner full letters,שין: בית,תיו ,the שבת,the inner letters יו,ית,ין,has the numerical value of 486, 16+410 +16=486, equal to the numerical value of the inner letters of the full letter of the word לב: למד בית,412+74 =486.

The knowledge of man removes from his heart, doubts which are the cause of lack of Joy and Happiness, in man's life.

Keeping the Shabbath properly, instills in man's heart Joy and Happiness in his life.

Shabbath, the day of thought, is the source of our ability to serve GOD with Joy, which is the way of serving GOD.

In fact, the same letters that spell the word "thought", מחשבה, when arranged in different order, spell the בשמחה"", "with joy".

The numerical value of the word "Thought" - מחשבה, is 355, has its source in the sphere of מלכות – Kingship , which is manifested in the lower world on the Shabbath.

The number 355 is the numerical value of the word ספירה Sphere. The sphere of מלכות - Kingship, is the last Sphere in tree of life, where all the Spheres are collected, this sphere, which is the starting point of its activities, in the world.

The same, is with the Shabbath, the source of the whole blessings in the six days of the week.

As the letters of the word, תגא follow those of the word, שבת we find support for what is written in the mystical books that on Shabbath according to the Kabbalah, the children of Israel deserving of the spiritual crowns which they merited at the time of the giving of the Torah, but which were taken away from them, after the sin of the golden calf and remained only with Moses.

SATISFACTION AND JOY ON THE SABBATH

On the Holy Shabbath, two fundamental concepts are revealed. which are indicated in the letters of names of numbers. Number five, חמשה , have the same letters, in a different order, of the word שמחה"" "Joy".

The umber seven letters שבע, by putting the dot on the left side of the letter ש will be the word שבע, satietyשבע, basically is a word which represent satisfaction.

On the connection of the number שבע- seven, and satisfied ,שבע says Rabbi Shimshon Rephael Hirash, that the number seven represent completion, seven days in the week, seven notes in the musical scale, etc.

Satisfaction - שבע, and חמשה - joy, a man merits by keeping the Shabbath. All this is alluded to in the Morning prayer of the Shabbath, where we say,"ישמחו במלכותך שומרי שבת וקוראי ענג , כולם ישבעו ויתענגו מטובך" " They rejoice in Your kingship, All of them are satiated and receive pleasure from Your goodness" .

Here we find these same concepts in verb form: ישמחו (they rejoice) corresponding to the number five- חמשה and ישבעו (they are satiated) corresponding to the number שבע,- Seven.

The lettersשבע ,- ז and the letter חמשה ה-, build the Hebrew word This-.זה The Hebrew word זה represent clear sight, as we find in many places in the Midrash, Shabbath is a day when the Light of GOD exist, as we saw before.

According to the Maharal of Prague, the number twelve expresses the concept of completion or perfection.

The Maharal of Prague explains that this is the cause it represent the four directions when each direction is complete in all three dimensions: length, breadth, and height.

TWO LOAVES OF BREAD ON SABBATH MEALS

The concept of perfection on the Shabbath, as represented by the number twelve, is also manifested in the twelve loaves of the לחם, הפנים,, the Face- Bread, which were placed on the Table, in the Temple Sanctuary, every Shabbath. By the merit of these twelve loaves the world remains in existence.

> According to the practice of the holy Ari, Rabbi Isaac Luria, this is the number of loaves used for the Shabbath meal in every Jewish home, twelve loaves corresponding to the Face-Bread which draws down abundance to this world,

The Face -Bread drew down an outpouring of blessing from the upper worlds to this world, through the twelve constellations.

On the Holy Shabbath, when the light of GOD presence is revealed to the Jewish people, who keep the Shabbath joy, as King David says in his psalm,(16,11) "There is satiety of joy in your Presence" "שבע שמחות את פניך",

It is Interesting to note, that our Sages in the Midrash Vyikra Rabba; say on the word, שבע, meaning satiated, to read it שבע , with the dot on the right side of the letter.

Seven, against the seven commandments of the festival of Succot, a festival full of Joy and happiness.

As noted, before, the Shabbath the seventh day, is connected with the sphere of kingship. Likewise, the Shabbath is connected with all of the letters of the Hebrew Alphabet.

This is revealed through the numerical value of the word ,שבת Shabbath, 702,which equals 27X26,where 27 is the total number of the letters in the Hebrew alfabet (including the five ,final forms ך,ם,ן,ף,ץ)).while twenty six, is the numerical value of the name of GOD , י-ה-ו-ה.

The numerical value of the word שבת - Shabbath 702, indicates that the Shabbath is connected with the seventh sphere, in the high world, the world of creation, which has to do with hundreds, (units, and tens, numbers which are connected with the worlds of action. and formation) according to the Kabbalah,

The number 2 , in 702, indicate to sphere of בינה, understanding, the second sphere after the sphere of חכמה -wisdom, as the Zohar says, that the Shabbath is connected with the spheres of בינה , understanding, and the sphere of מלכות–Kingship.

Every Shabbath, Moses grants Israel the privilege of these crowns. On the Shabbath, when the illumination from these crowns falls on the faces of the Children of Israel, it gives them a totally new soul.

EXTRA SOUL ON THE SABBATH

This is why our sages tell us, that although it is customary to have a new guest at each recitation of the Seven Blessings during the week of celebration, in honor of a bride and groom, on Shabbath no such "new face" is required.

"וביום השביעי שבת וינפש", "on the seventh day He ceased to work and rested". The word וינפש (and rested) is a combination of וי (a loss) and נפש (soul), indicating, according to many commentaries, the sorrow of a man on the end of the Shabbath (the departing of Shabbath) when he feels the loss of his extra soul.

It is precisely when this extra soul is removed that man realizes the extent of his loss. For this reason, on end of Shabbath, we are given spices to smell in order to strengthen and revitalize the soul that remains after the additional soul has departed.

Through this loss a man recognizes that he was indeed privileged to have an extra soul with him on Shabbath.

Thus, we see how the aforementioned verse relates the loss of the added soul to Shabbath itself.

A different explanation of the word וינפש , is possible, if we apply our earlier description of the word שבת as being assembled from שב and ת , implying the breaking of lust on Shabbath.

As is generally known, the נפש is the lower spiritual entity of man, after the רוח and the נשמה. .

This animalistic נפש, as it were, disappears on the Shabbath, because all desires are elevated through true intellectual judgment and introspection, and one feels disgrace for the animalistic actions of the weekdays.

The Divine Light which rests on man during the Shabbath dissipates his materialistic נפש, desires and awakens in him shame at having these desires; it brings him to repentance, as we saw before from the implications of the word Shabbath.

The holy Zohar states (Yitro, 88b): "Shabbath is the name of the Holy One, blessed is He, which is peace in every dimension." Bnei Yissachar explains (Ma'amarei HaShabbat, ma'amar 1):

" The twenty-seven letters of the Hebrew alphabet lie., including the five final forms, ך ם ן ף ץ, are the letters with which the universe was created, by the power of the divine Name which permeates the letters".

Now, G-d created the worlds in six days, while the Shabbath, the Seventh Day, is the aspect of form which perfects the material.

This is seen in the numerical value of the phrase, 'this is the soul (Neshamah) of the material"702 -" ,זה הנשמה אל החומר, which equals the numerical value of the word, Shabbat (702, שבת).

THE SABBATH GIVE FORM THE WORLD

The concept of "form" (צורה, 301) partakes of the nature of "fire" (אש, 301), for fire gives form to the material (as when metal is heated for hammering or melted for molding). The fire of the Shabbath gives form to the other, non-sacred days.

Just as the Shabbath gives form to the materiality of the weekdays, so too does Israel give form to the materiality of the other nations.

Just as the purpose and special power of the Sabbath is to give form to the weekdays, so too the purpose and special power of Israel is to give form to humanity.

This is why the passage "And the heavens and the earth were completed..." is the only place in the Torah where the name "Israel" is encoded at intervals of fifty letters.

There are forty-nine letters in this verse which summarizes the account of the creation.

The tradition of writing a Torah scroll tells us that in this verse the letter ה numerical value (5) in the word בהבראם (meaning "when they were created") is to be written smaller than the other letters. Not counting this small ה, there are forty-nine letters in this verse

THE NUMBER 49 -7X7 AND THE SABBATH

Forty-nine, being seven times seven, represents the perfection of the concept of "seven." This same number of letters, forty-nine, appears again in a passage where the Torah commands Sabbath observance as an eternal sign between the Holy One, blessed is He, and the Nation of Israel.

The final forty-nine Hebrew letters of that passage read: "For in six days G-d made the heavens and the earth, and on the seventh day He ceased and rested" " וביום השביעי שבת וינפש".

Why is the number of verses in the entire account of Creation (35) equal to the number of letters in the verse describing the first Sabbath, "And the heavens and the earth were completed.. "

This emphasizes the connection between the creation of the universe and the Shabbath, which our Sages (in the wording of the Shabbath night Kiddush) called: "a commemorate ion of the act of creation."

The special powers of the Shabbath, are alluded to through the code language of letters skip before the passage "And the heaven and the earth were completed ....."

The letter ת in the verse, "וירא אל-הים, את" before this verse, is the last of the letter skip of the word ברית, every thirteen letters. interesting to note,that there are only twice in Genesis, the appearance of the word ברית (in a letter skip of thirteen.

Thirteen, is very important number in Judaism, most important, being the numerical value of the words אחד indicate to one GOD, and the numerical value of the word אהבה , indicating to the love of GOD.

The Staff of Sabbath

In pronunciation, the word Shabbath שבת is similar to the word שבט. Their similarity lies in the letters ת and ט, which are interchangeable, since both belong to the group of letters which are enunciated with the tongue (ד.ט.ל.נ.ת). שבט means a rod or staff with which one leads, steers or punishes, and it appears in the Holy Scriptures many times in this context.

The word שבט, is constructed from word שב and the letter ט. The letter ט, according to book Letters of Rabbi Akiva, is pronounced טית (tet), which is similar to the word טיט (mortar, clay).

Therefore connotes material grossness. Thus, we derive that; שבט is the breaking off (שב) from the material world (ט).

The שבט is the instrument of severance from materialism, just as שבת has the power to terminate materialistic lust symbolized by the letter ת.

Even though they belong to the same group, the letter ת is articulated more softly than the letter, ט in order to teach us that materialism is the state of powerful lust.

The stronger pronunciation of a letter, indicates an increased strength in the meaning of the word itself, an example being the words in תאוה (lust) and תועבה (abomination).

The letters ע and ב, in, תועבה are stronger than the letters א and ו, in תאוה, indicating what happens when lust becomes stronger.

The Shabbath gives man a staff with which he can fight against the materialism of the secular weekdays.

The word שבט also indicates expansion and branching out.

In our mystical books it is written that the tribes of Israel (שבטי ישראל) are comparable to branches sprouting from their heavenly source and spreading out into the world.

It is worthwhile to note the closeness of the word שבט to the word שפט (to judge) since a rod is an instrument of punishment meted out by a judge.

Similarly, שפט contains the same letters as פשט (spreading out), teaching us that the Shabbath is a time of proliferation and distribution of God's holy forces in this world, and that these forces arouse man to judge his actions and evoke suffering in his soul, bringing him finally to total repentance.

Enjoying Sabbath Properly

The simplest definition of Sahbbath - שבת is cessation, hinting that through the workings of nature and the constellations the Shabbath is a negative and deprived day on which man feels depression and sadness.

This is the reason, commentators explain, for the mitzvah of שבת ענג (enjoyable activity on Shabbath). It is to show that the Jewish people are above the fortune dictated by the stars, and are not influenced by them.

In other languages Shabbath is named after the planet which influences destruction, שבתי - Saturn. Rabbi Jonathan Eybeschuetz said that for this reason the peoples of the world did not choose the Shabbath, as their day of rest.

Those who observe the Shabbath properly, elevate themselves, through its influence, above the decree of the stars. Those who do not observe the Shabbath, are given over to feelings of sadness and depression.

The difference between these two types is revealed in the word ענג (enjoyment), referring to the commandment of ענג שבת .

ענג – ENJOYMENT נגע - AGONY DISTRESS

Rearranging the letters ענג , we come up with נגע (plague, disaster), the complete opposite of ענג , as the book of formation says, "There is nothing higher than ענג, and nothing lower than נגע".

נגע , represents sorrow, agony, distress and loneliness. The relationship between ענג and נגע can be understood from a midrash which states that when Israel heard the Torah portion, dealing with נגעים, (plagues) they were terribly frightened, so God appeased them by relegating נגע to the other nations of the world, and ענג and happiness to Israel.

Plagues and disasters come in order to stimulate man to repent for his wicked actions. This method is required for those who are on a very low level and do not know the value of spirituality.

In one who is on a high spiritual level, the שבת ענג arouses lofty spiritual feelings which will bring him to despise his gross sinful deeds and devote himself to a pure, spiritual life.

ענג and נגע, are two ways in which man is brought closer to his Creator; those who are worthy achieve this closeness through ענג שבת while the materialistic minded achieve it through the suffering and anguish brought about by severe plagues.

The commandment to enjoy on Shabbath, mainly is by the three meals that we have on Shabath. These three meals correspond to the three Patrriachs, Abraham; Issac and Jacob.

Each of the Patriarchs is associated with one of the three Divine attribute mention above. Abraham with חסד Loving kindness ,Isaac with גבורה strength, Jacob with רחמים Mercy.

The three meals of the Shabbath are also associated with certain Kabbalistic concepts.

The evening meals associated with the Holy Apple trees ,which is identical with the sphere of מלכות Kingship, the morning meal is associated with the Ancient Holy one,(Atika Kadisha)while the third meal is associated with small Countenance(Zeir anpin).

ענג(enjoyment), in contrast to שמחה (happiness), is dependent upon the intellect and mind, while , שמחה is dependent upon the heart.

The relationship between the Shabbath and the other Jewish holidays, is comparable to the relationship between the mind, and the heart.

The mitzvah of ענגis specially ascribed to Shabbath, whereas the mitzvah of שמחה is linked with the holidays.

THE SABBATH AND THE MIND

The connection between Shabbath and the mind is clear, when we consider the relationship of the letters שבת, to the letters ראש , which we described above.

ענג , according to the Zohar, is comprised of the first letters of the words עדן נהר גן (Eden, river, and garden) which appear in the Torah in the verse "ונהר יוצא מעדן להשקות את הגן" ("And a river went forth from Eden to water the garden").

Eden symbolizes the upper world, the source of abundance and blessing which are transmitted via the river to the garden, a symbol for the Community of Israel - as indicated by the verse in Song of Songs, "A sealed garden is my sister-bride."

Because of this ענג,, the children of Israel are privileged with the three meals of the Shabbath day.

As is written in the mystical books, each meal corresponds to one of the three fathers, for each father was perfect in a particular characteristic: Abraham, in loving-kindness, Isaac, in strength, and Jacob, in glory.

As is known that the שבת - Shabbath is "מעין עולם הבא","like the world to come", as is written (Mechilta d'Rabbi Yishmael (13:31)

" .. It is, therefore, written "to know that I, the Lord, etc."

I spoke only of one who has knowledge (to internalize this.) "That I, the Lord, sanctify you":

In the "world to come", as with the" sanctity of the Sabbath" in this world — whence we derive that the sanctity of Shabbath is of a kind with that of the world to come.

And thus, is it written (psalm 92) " A song; for the Sabbath day. It is good to praise the LORD, to sing hymns to Your name, O Most High, to proclaim Your steadfast love at daybreak".

THE LETTER ת THE WORLD TO COME

This quality of the Shabbath, can be analyzed from the word Shabbath- שבת as שב –ת. The letter ת the last letter in the alphabet, according to the Kabbalah, represents the world to come.

The number 400, the numerical value of the letter ת, representing world to come, based on the number 4, indicates to four directions, as our world is built on three dimension.

Also, the shape of the letter ת, looks like somebody whose foot is on the way to go out.

The word שב, is a form of the word (שוב) return, thus the letters שב – ת, indicate that on the Shabbath, the Jewish person returns שב, to the source of his soul, i.e. "The world to come" (ת).

On the Shabbath, the Jewish person is attached to the world to come as the Maharal of Prague states (Chidushei Agadot on Shabat, 118).

This is what Mahral says, "One who makes the Shabbath pleasurable, attaches himself to the World to Come, (Berachot, 57,b)and the pleasure of the Shabbath of the Shabbath is a semblance of the World To Come, which is all pleasure and goodness.

Therefore one who keeps the Shabbath, is given a boundless inheritance, since he becomes attached to the world to come which is boundless and infinite. .

THE NUMBER 9 AND THE SABBATH

The Upper World represented by the number 9. a number which represents Truth and Eternity, as we saw before, is symbolized by the circle on the top.

This is in contrast to the number 6, with the circle at the bottom, representing our Lower World with its six ordinary weekdays.

Friday evening meal of the Shabbath, is related to Isaac, the element of strength, being the counterpart of the phrase, "Keep the Shabbath day", since with the end of the ordinary weekdays and the entering of the Shabbath, the man is required to overcome the secular atmosphere which he has just left, and careful watch is necessary so that the sanctity of Shabbath is not marred.

The morning meal of Shabbath is called the feast of the Highest Divinity, corresponding to "Remember the Shabbath day to keep it holy," and is identified with our forefather Abraham.

At this time of the Shabbath day, the Divine blessings - ברכה; abundantly from the Source of all blessings.

The word for "remember" is זכר, which is numerically equivalent to 227, the same value as the word ברכה (blessing).

The third meal of the Shabbath corresponds to Jacob, the attribute of glory. Unites the loving-kindness of Abraham, and the strength of Isaac.

This explains the universal custom of calling this final meal, "the feast of the three feasts," because it does in fact combine all three meals of the Shabbath.

The Remarkable שׁ

The holiness of our three fathers which descends on the Children of Israel on Shabbath, is revealed, according to the Zohar, in the breaking down of the word שבת, into the components שׁ and בת.

The letter שׁ with its three branches, hints at the three forfathers Abrahm, Isaac and Jacob, while the word בת (daughter) is one of the names by which the Community of Israel is called in the Holy Scriptures.

Upon closer inspection of the three branches of the letter שׁ, is discovered that each branch is a different letter, the letters ז י ו, which form the Hebrew word, זיו meaning splendor to do with the Shabbath.

The branch to the right forms the letter, י the middle branch forms the letter ו, and the branch to the left forms ז.

These three letters, symbolize our forefathers. The letter י on the right branch of the שׁ , stands for the spiritual powers of Abraham which come to rest on the Children of Israel on Shabbath.

The letter י is related to Abraham, since it is the letter which signifies wisdom. This trait characterizes Abraham who, through the power of wisdom, recognized his Creator.

Also, as our mystical books tell us, wisdom and loving-kindness have a common connection in that both belong to the right side. opposite understanding and strength which are on the left.

On the left-hand side of the letter שׁ stands the letter ז, the letter which symbolizes a weapon of war and might, and which, in its written form, resembles the shape of a sword.

This is Isaac, a pillar of strength, the attribute of the left side. The letter ו, formed by the middle branch of the שׁ, signifies אמת (truth), and it is this letter, according to the Zohar, which God set upon Cain.

This quality of אמת is attributed to Jacob who possessed, as the word itself suggests, all other qualities from א to ת.

The letter ש, as stated often in the Zohar, is called the letter of truth, truth which is conveyed by the harmony of the three branches.

This being so, we can deduce that the word שבת indicates the joining of the quality of truth to the בת, the children of Israel, on Shabbath, and it influences even the common layman not to lie on Shabbath.

With the coming of Shabbath the creation of the world was completed.

THE NUMBER THREE IN THE CREATION

The number three represent the three Patriarchs, who are the foundation of the world's existence. Our sages teach in the Ethics of the Fathers ((1:2): "The world stands on three things, on the Torah, on the service of GOD, and on the acts of kindness".

These three things are epitomize by the three patriarchs.

Jacob epitomizes Torah, Isaac, and service, and Abraham, kindness.

At the end of this chapter, we find similar dictum of our sages" The world exists by virtue of three things, Justice, Truth, and Peace".

These things also are epitomized by the three patriarchs, Isaac epitomize Justice, Jacob, Truth, Abraham Peace.

Thus, the number three (שלשה) is the foundation of the world.

This fact is encoded in the first verse of the Torah, "בראשית ברא א-ל-הים את השמים ואת הארץ" "In the beginning GOD created the heaven and the earth."

If we begin from the first letter ש, we find the word, שלשה three, in letter skip of seven.

This teaches us that the principal of three is built up by means of the principal of seven, which correspond to the seventh day.

The idea of the number three, which completes seven, making a total of ten, is revealed in the Holy Zohar,(Part 3,page,273):

"One must eat three meals on Shabbath, for this completes the seven benedictions of the prayers (the Amida prayers on the Sabbath contains seven benedictions) bringing them to the perfection of ten."

From this we see that the three meals of the Shabbath, are considered equal in importance to the seven benedictions of the Shabbath prayers.

The relationship of Israel to the Shabbath being the foundation of the world, come out from a Midrash Rabbah (11:12) Rabbi Shimon bar Yochai (his name שמעון בר יוחי has the numerical value 702, which equal to the word of שבת shabbath).

Rabbi Shiman bar Yochai stated: The Shabbath said to the Holy One, blessed is He, everything has a mate, but I have no mate.

The Holy one is He, said to her, the congregation of Israel Is your mate.

The partnership between Israel and the Shabbath, is a precondition for the tractate, Shabbath, "Whoever cites the existence of the universe, as the Talmud says in Kidush on the eve of the Shabbath, saying, "And the heavens and the earth were completed...." it is as if he was a partner with the holy One bless be He in the creation of the universe.

This partnership, says the holy Or Hachim, is expressed in the fact, that the words used by the Torah to describe this are -ברא א-להים לעשות," the last letters of these words spelling אמת, the connection between שבת and אמת .

Thus, truth is permanently established in the world with the Shabbath. The entire world's existence is dependent on truth, and without it the world is destined for annihilation.

TRUTH THE BASIS OF EXISTENCE OF THE WORLD

That the creation of the world was also dependent upon truth is suggested by the last letters of the first words of the Torah, "בראשית ברא א-להים" ("In the beginning God created ").

Although here the letters are not in the proper order to spell אמת, as was the case with ברא א-להים לעשות , even this fact contains a lesson for us -namely that only with the creation of the Shabbath, is truth established in the world.

According to the Orach Chaim and the masters of Kabbalah, the Creation in essence was only six days, as the Torah verse tells us, "Six days God made the heavens and the earth."

"Six days", the verse says, and not "In six days," informing us that the Creation in its essence was those six days and that afterward came Shabbath came to give strength to the world and establish it; and the cycle continues.

If God forbid will not be anyone observing the Shabbath in the world, the world will return to void and nothing.

Truth, concealed in the Shabbath, constitutes the founding element of the world and allows the world to exist.

Shabbath, as the basis and foundation of the world's existence, can also be seen by arranging the letters , שבת into שת and ב. בית ,ת.

שת, meaning foundation, and ב stands for בית house, alluding to the structure of the world. שבת then, is the foundation and existence of the world.

As we saw above, the word בראשית symbolizes the essence of the foundation of the world, according to the Zohar.

This same word, indicates to us, that the process was completed in six days, since we can divide it into the wordsברא שית , which means, "created in six." (שית, in Aramaic, means six).

This refers to the six days of doing work. The same letters, as we saw above, can be transposed to form ירא שבת (fear of the Shabbath), showing that this concept is dependent on the first one mentioned.

Therefore, we can conclude that the existence of the six days of work is dependent on the fear of Shabbath.

There is another aspect to the letter, ש that we find in mystical writings, which fits in with our previous explanation of the value of Shabbath.

The letter ש, which is pronounced שין (shin), comes from the term שן (sharp, keen), referring to the power of understanding as stated in the verse " ושיננתם לבניך ("And you shall teach them to your sons").

This phrase emphasizes, that the words of Torah should be keen in our mouths, after we develop proper understanding of them. Therefore, the letter , שcomes to let us know, that man is graced with additional understanding on Shabbath along with the additional soul.

The Attributes of the Sabbath

The relatedness of the extra soul to the extra understanding, is expressed in the fact that understanding is the eighth attribute after the seven main attributes, and the same is true for the soul which dwells in the mind and is therefore connected to understanding, as the verse states,"ונשמת ש-די תבינם ("and the soul of the Almighty which gives them understanding").

The letters of נשמה (soul) are the same as those in שמנה (eight), making us aware of the connection between the soul and the eighth attribute, and understanding.

On the Shabbath, man understands of the significance of life and the world, is much deeper than on ordinary weekdays, and brings him to a proper intellectual evaluation of his place in the world.

The power of understanding is also bound with fear, an attribute which is also increased on the Shabbath, as we saw above. The attribute of fear is related to might.

The bolstering of oneself against the evil inclination is a function of fear of Heaven.

This kinship appears in the numerical value of גבורה (might) and יראה (fear). Each word is equal to 216.

Understanding and might belong, mystically speaking, to the left side of the attributes, opposite wisdom and loving-kindness on the right. אימה (awe) expresses the distant fear one feels when the object of his fear is far away.

This type of fear is related to בינה (understanding) because the letter א and the letter מ in, אימה which are its main letters, precede the main letters of בינה, the letter מ . and the letter נ.

Thus, awe and understanding on the Shabbath are interlocked with each other and instill in man deep appreciation for the value of life.

The letter ש also expresses the idea of unity, illustrated by the harmony of the branches and their union at their root. In the same way, the Shabbath, unites the Children of Israel, as the Zohar says in its elaboration on the Torah, "The secret of Shabbath which is united in the secret of oneness."

The ability of the Shabbath, to create unity within Israel derives from the fact that on Shabbath the souls of the children of Israel ascend to their heavenly roots, where they all unite; for all souls of Israel have the same source, and only the material world separates and distinguishes them.

This coming together of the souls at their mutual source unites Israel with the upper world, the world of oneness, as the Zohar says, "In the same way they unite in the upper world, so the Jewish people unite in the lower world."

THE SABBATH DAY OF UNITY

Just as total unity prevails in the upper realms, so does it prevail in this world on Shabbath.

The joining of the souls of Israel at their common root on the Shabbath, is also evident if we divide the word שבת, into, ש and. ב

The letter, ש symbolizes the root, as the form of the letter clearly indicates, and בתis Israel, whose souls unite at this root on the Shabbath.

The root of all Jewish souls is dependent also upon the three fathers, each branch of the ש representing one of the three fathers, as we saw above.

The letterש, according to the Book of Creation, (related to our for forefather Abraham) is the letter which indicates to the element of אש (fire).

As we saw above, the letter ש also represents understanding linked with strength, strength being dependent upon the element of fire.

The relationship of the letter שto strength, is noticeable in the pronunciation שין (shin), which is similar to שן (shayn). שן in the Holy Scriptures often symbolizes a fighting instrument, or weapon and the strength of a people, as in, for example,"שיני רשעים שברת" ("The might of the wicked you have broken").

Fire is the highest of the four basic elements, fire, wind, water and earth. בת, the daughter Israel, is connected to the spiritual fire which glows on Shabbath from the purifying and refining of the Jewish souls.

The connection of שבת to the element of אשis expressed through the letters ת being those which follow אשin the order of the alphabet.

The element of fire on the Shabbath instills into the hearts of the children Israel, the fire of fear, a fire channeled from the brilliant Divine Light.

This fact is emphasized by the letters of) fire אש and אר(light). The letter ר of, ארprecedes the letter ש of , , אשand informs us that the element of light, is clothed in the garment of fire, and that it illuminates for man the way of truth in the world.

With this spiritual fire the Torah was written, for as our sages say, the Divine fire is concealed within the Shabbath, and Shabbath is considered equal to the whole of Torah.

On Shabbath the Torah was given to Israel, so the sanctity of the Torah was united with the sanctity of Israel within the sanctity of Shabbath.

The light of the Torah was revealed in such a way that the awe of Heaven would become securely situated in the hearts of Israel, as the verse says (Exodus 20:17),

"In order that the awe of Him will be upon you, so that you will not sin." The awe spoken about, say the Sages, is shame. The concept of יראה (ir'ah, "awe") in essence means האָרה (he'arah, "illumination" of the heart, and this is the essence of shame.

Even though that the better part of the preparation for the Sabbath is concentrated on Friday, it actually begins three days prior to the Sabbath, as our Sages tell us (Bamidbar Rabbah).

Sabbath: The Spiritual Healer

Shabbath is the foundation of the world to come, and those who enjoy it properly earn for themselves the experience of eternal life and of total purity and truth. On Shabbath the soul attaches itself to the original source of eternal life from which it came.

This is the point which our mystical books acknowledge when they tell us that the letter ת , the last letter of the alphabet, indicates the world to come.

For this reason, writes Rabbi Tzadok Hakohen, when the Talmud deals with matters of this world it uses the number 300 and not 400 (400 is the numerical value of (ת).

שhas a numerical value of 300, indicating to the three dimensions of this world, but the letter ת, is equal to 400 and represents the four dimensions which are present in the world to come.

According to the Book of Creation, Shabbath, which is of the essence of the world to come, is created through the letter, ת the letter which symbolizes the world to come.

The return of the soul to its source in the world to come, is revealed through the construction of שבת from שב andת .

This indicates to the שיבה (returning) of the soul to ת (the world to come).

The soul returns to its source and clings to it, but all this is dependent upon the ability of man to abolish.

(שב) his lustful instinct (ת) on Shabbath, as we saw above.

To recognize the heavenly origins of the Shabbath , we have only to look at its numerical value of the word 702- שבת, or expressed differently, 700 + 2.

The number 700 represents the lofty source of the 7 days of Creation, because as the Kabbalah tells us about these numbers.

The units of hundreds, tens, and ones designate the upper worlds, the hundreds being higher worlds than the tens, and the tens being higher worlds than the ones.

THE NUMBER 7-2 AND THE SABBATH

About the holy 72-letter name of God, the Zohar says that there are 70 main letters and the other 2 serve as witnesses. The same can be said about שבת , that it is essentially the channel of emanations from the upper worlds (represented by 700) and the witnesses to this process (represented by 2).

The fire of Shabbath devours the fire of pride, lust, and jealousy. Each of these characteristics is compared to fire in many texts, and it is explained that pride, lust and jealousy are three negative forces which Abraham, Isaac, and Jacob fought against.

Abraham battled lust with his loving-kindness and devotion; Isaac combated pride, the root of idol worship, by offering himself unconditionally to God; while Jacob, the man of truth and peace, fought jealousy and bloodshed.

The pure, holy fire of the three fathers which burns on Shabbath consumes and nullifies the evil fires which oppose them, and the harmful roots are laid to rest.

This is another property of the Shabbath revealed through the letters שבת. The word שבת means "laid to rest," and the letters שבת are clearly seen to be its root, thereby describing the ability of Shabbath to lay the destructive influences to rest.

The three heavenly fires of holiness have a connection with the different names attributed to God.

The name of God י-ה-ו-ה symbolizes mercy and loving-kindness, while the name of -אדנ-י (mastership)

pertains to judgment and אדנות.

(It is forbidden to write the name of God needlessly; therefore the letter ק is substituted for the letter ה. In computing the numerical value, however, we use the value of ה. The same is true for the name אלקים.)

Torah is the aspect of אמת (truth), the quality of Jacob, which includes everything from the letter א to the letter ת .

The numerical value of the two above-mentioned names, together with the numerical value of תורה (Torah) is 702. As pointed out in Bnei Yissaschar, this is the same numerical value asשבת.

This confirms the words of the Zohar which state that שבתis one of the names of God. The computation of numerical values is as follows:

$$י-ה-ו -ה=26$$
$$אדני=65$$
$$תורה=611$$

———-

702

As our sages teach, on an esoteric level, the Torah is composed entirely of the names of God, and is related to the qualities of Jacob who "dwelled in tents," the tents of Torah and prayer. One combination of names of God which has the same numerical values as שבת is the combination אהיה י-ה-ו-ה הקדוש ברוך הוא . The computation is:

$$אהיה=21$$
$$י=ה – ו -ה=26$$
$$הקדוש ברוך הוא=655$$

—————

שבת=702

According to mystical writings, the first three letters

ו-ה-י-" in the name pip' allude to the qualities of 1) wisdom or loving-kindness, 2) strength or understanding, and 3) knowledge or glory. These are all qualities of the three fathers.

On the Shabbath the world is showered with heavenly abundance from those upper worlds which have a strong tie with the letters of this name of God. This nana (blessing) coming from the upper worlds is illustrated by Bnei Yissaschar, in the following computation of numerical values:

$$227+10 \text{ ברכה}+\text{י}$$
$$227+5 \text{ ברכה}+\text{ה}$$
$$227+6 \text{ ברכה}+\text{ו}$$

————-

$$\text{שבת}=702$$

The blessing from these three upper worlds is stored in Shabbath, and through this blessing all the other days are blessed.

Preparing for Sabbath

The preparation for Shabbath already begins on Friday, for as our mystical books tell us, it is incumbent upon man to repent on Friday for all the evil actions which he did during the week, and then he will deserve to receive holiness into his heart.

Referring to this spiritual preparation is the verse "And the Children of Israel shall keep the Shabbath for all their generations."

The word for generations, דרתם, according to the Zohar, comes from the word דירה (dwelling place), and its purpose in this verse is to remind us to prepare a dwelling place in our hearts for the holiness of Shabbath.

This is accomplished by proper repentance on the day before Shabbath. In light of this concept, we note that the letters תשבה (repentance) are the same letters as השבת (the Shabbath) and also as בשת (shame, disgrace), teaching us that through repentance and shame for sinful deeds, a space for the sanctity of Shabbath is placed within man on weekdays.

After the Shabbath arrives, the spiritual feeling is fortified and brings man to full and perfect repentance.

The recognition by man of his place in the world on the Shabbath is, according to Chidushei HaRim, indicated by the prohibition of leaving the fixed boundaries on Shabbath, as the verse says, "A man shall not go out from his place on Shabbath."

The great shame which a man feels for the sins he has committed is due to the Shabbath light.

This light evokes shame in a person for his actions. The idea is revealed by the letters ב ש ת (shame) which immediately follow the letters אר (light) in the order of the alphabet.

This relationship explains the words of our sages who said that the characteristic shame is planted in the souls of Jews from the time of the giving of the Torah.

Of this experience it is said that it was done in such a way that the fear of Heaven would become securely fixed in the hearts of Israel, as the verse says, "In order that the fear of Him shall be upon you."

The fear spoken about, say our sages is shame. "יראה" (fear) in essence is ראיה (illumination) of the heart, and this is the essence of shame.

Even though the better part of the preparation for Shabbath is concentrated on Friday, it actually begins three days prior to Shabbath, as our sages tell us, "Three days before the the Shabbath emerges from its majestic abode."

During these three days a man makes himself ritually fit to merit the Divine illumination of the three fathers, which illuminations are embodied in the three branches of the ש .

These three days provide a preparation period for the three parts of the soul נפש, רוח and נשמה. . The נפש resides in the liver, the רוח in the heart, and the נשמה in the brain.

About the Heart in which the רוח dwells, says the Tikuney Zoar (Tikun 24, page 69 b) that the Shbath and the heart, are connected, as the Shabbath in the world is like the heart in the body.

HEART IN MAN SABBATH HEART OF TIME

The connection of the Heart ‎לב- and the Shbbath , ‎שבת-is indicted in the numerical value of the of the full writings of the letter.

The full letters of the word heart- ‎לב- are, 486- ‎למד בית ,the full writing of the letters of the word ‎שבת are ‎ש ין ב ית, ת יו the inner letters ‎יו ית ין have the numerical value 486, as the full letters of the word ‎לב- heart.

The reason that in the letters ‎שבת we take the inner full numerical value is that the connection of the Shabbath to the heart is in the depth of the Holiness of Sabbath.

The‎מלכות -Kingship, is the heart of the nation. Analog us to the Heart, an all encompassing organ the unites the entire person limbs. That is the light force which come from a higher realm

In the human being is the King, and like this says Rabbi Shimshon Pincus it in his book (Shabat malketa, p41) that is as the heart unites all the limbs of the body, so the Shabbath the king, unites the Jewish people and brings peace among them

Taking the first letters of the Hebrew names for liver (‎כבד), heart (‎לב), and brain (‎מח) produces the word ‎כלם(vessels), revealing that the three different parts of the soul are the vessels intended to contain the holiness of Shabbath.

The heavens, the earth, and all their hosts represent in this world the three divisions of the soul. Thus we can understand the words of our mystical books which say that the universe is likened to a huge man, and man is like a miniature universe.

About the verse (And the heavens and the earth and all their hosts were finished, the early scholars remark that the word ‎ויכלו (finished) is from the term ‎כלם (vessels) and indicates that the heavens and the earth were made to be vessels for receiving the sanctity of Shabbath.

Therefore, the task of man is to prepare in himself the vessels which will receive this sanctity.

ABRAHAM ISAAC AND JACOB AND THE SABBATH

Abraham, Isaac, and Jacob fought against the evil forces. Abraham battled lust with his loving-kindness and devotion; Isaac combated pride, the root of idol worship, by offering himself unconditionally to God; while Jacob, the man of truth and peace, fought jealousy and bloodshed.

The pure, holy fire of the three fathers which burns on Shabbath consumes and nullifies the evil fires which oppose them, and the harmful roots are laid to rest.

This is another property of Shabbath revealed through the letters שבת. The word שבת means "laid to rest," and the letters שבת are clearly seen to be its root, thereby describing the ability of Shabbath to lay the destructive influences to rest.

The three heavenly fires of holiness have a connection with the different names attributed to God. The name of God י-ק-ו-ק * symbolizes mercy and loving-kindness, while the name of אדנ-י (mastership) pertains to judgment and אדנות.

The Torah is the aspect of אמת (truth), the quality of Jacob, which includes everything from א to ת. The numerical value of the two above-mentioned names, together with the numerical value of תורה (Torah) is 702.

As pointed out in Bnei Yissaschar, this is the same numerical value as שבת..

This confirms the words of the Zohar which state that שבת is one of the names of God. The computation of numerical values is as follows:

$$\text{י-ה-ו-ה} = 26$$
$$\text{אדני} = 65$$
$$\text{תורה} = 611$$

———-

702

As our sages teach, on an esoteric level, the Torah is composed entirely of the names of God, and is related to the qualities of Jacob who "dwelled in tents," the tents of Torah and prayer. One combination of names of God which has the same numerical values as שבת is the combination אהיה י-ה-ו-ה הקדוש ברוך הוא. The computation is:

אהיה=21

י=ה- ו –ה=26

הקדוש ברוך הוא=655

———————

שבת=702

PREPARING FOR SABBATH

The preparation for Shabbath already begins on Friday, for as our mystical books tell us, it is incumbent upon man to repent on Friday for all the evil actions which he did during the week, and then he will deserve to receive holiness into his heart.

Referring to this spiritual preparation is the verse "And the Children of Israel shall keep the Shabbath for all their generations."

The word for generations, דרתם, according to the Zohar comes from the word דירה (dwelling place), and its purpose in this verse is to remind us to prepare a dwelling place in our hearts for the holiness of Shabbath.

This is accomplished by proper repentance on the day before Shabbath. In light of this concept, we note that the letters תשבה (repentance) are the same letters as השבת (the Shabbath) and also as בשת (shame, disgrace), teaching us that through repentance and shame for sinful deeds, a space for the sanctity of Shabbath is placed within man on weekdays.

After the Shabbath arrives, the spiritual feeling is fortified and brings man to full and perfect repentance.

The recognition by man of his place in the world on Shabbath is, according to Chidushei HaRim, indicated by the prohibition of leaving the fixed boundaries on Shabbath, as the verse says, "A man shall not go out from his place on Shabbath."

The great shame which a man feels for the sins he has committed is due to the Shabbath light. This light evokes shame in a person for his actions.

The idea is revealed by the letters בש ת (shame) which immediately follow אר light) in the order of the alphabet.

This relationship explains the words of our sages who said that the characteristic shame is planted in the souls of Jews from the time of the giving of the Torah.

Of this experience it is said that it was done in such a way that the fear of Heaven would become securely fixed in the hearts of Israel, as the verse says, "In order that the fear of Him shall be upon you." The fear spoken about, say, our sages is shame. "יראה" (fear) in essence is ראיה (illumination) of the heart, and this is the essence of shame.

Even though the better part of the preparation for Shabbath is concentrated on Friday, it actually begins three days prior to Shabbath, as our sages tell us, "Three days before Shabbath, Shabbath emerges from its majestic abode."

During these three days a man makes himself ritually fit to merit the Divine illumination of the three fathers, which illuminations are embodied in the three branches of the ש .

THE LAST THREE DAYS OF THE WEEK PREPARE FOR THE SABBATH

These three days provide a preparation period for the three parts of the soul נפש, רוח andנשמה .

The נפש resides in the liver, the רוח in the heart, and the נשמה in the brain.

As we saw before Taking the first letters of the Hebrew names for liver (כבד), heart (לב), and brain (מח) produces the word כלם(vessels), revealing that the three different parts of the soul are the vessels intended to contain the holiness of Shabbath.

The heavens, the earth, and all their hosts represent in this world the three divisions of the soul.

Thus we can understand the words of our mystical books which say that the universe is likened to a huge man, and man is like a miniature universe.

About the verse (And the heavens and the earth and all their hosts were finished"'), the early scholars remark that the word ויכלו (finished) is from the term כלם (vessels) and indicates that the heavens and the earth were made to be vessels for receiving the sanctity of Shabbath. Therefore, the task of man is to prepare in himself the vessels which will receive this sanctity.

Interesting to note, that the numerical value of the words מח לב כבד, is 112 which is the same numerical value of the three names of GOD connected with the three spheres which are in the center, of the tree of life.

The three names of GOD, י- אדנ -ה-ו-ה-י– היה-א. The name –היה-א against the highest sphere in the tree of life, כתר -the crown. The name י-ה-ו-ה, the name of תפארת – splendor, in the middle of the tree, and the name of GOD י-אדנ, against מלכות kingship on the bottom of the Tree of life.

The number 112 is also the numerical value of GOD names א-להים the name the sphere of גבורה -strength and the name GOD י-ה-ו-ה the name of GOD the sphere which has to doרחמים – Mercy.

Part of the commandment of preparing for the Shabbath is took forward to it and year for it.

The Rambam writes in his Code of Law (Lwas of the Shabat30:2)that a person should forward to greeting the sabbath ,as if he were going forth to greet a king.

SABBATH, HOLINESS AND ROYALTY

The Sabbath is described as a day of rest, as we say in the Sabbath afternoon prayers, "A Day of rest and holiness You gave to Your people." This rest means being mentally and physically settled, resulting in expanded consciousness. The root of מנוחה (menuchah, "rest" is נח.

The same letters in reverse order spell חן (chen, "grace"), indicating an expression of the lamp of wisdom since in are the initial letters of the words חכמת נסתר (Chochmat Hanistar,

"The Hidden Wisdom," i.e., the Kabbalah). Man's whole being is imbued with the in (chen, "grace") flowing forth from this lamp of wisdom, and because of this he is able to attain complete and perfect rest.

The word מח (mo'ach, "brain") is similar to נח (no'ach, "rest"), the letter נ following מ in the Hebrew alphabet.

These points out to us that true rest is dependent upon illumination of the mind. Similarly the word מנוח (manoach, "rest") contains the word מח (mo'ach, "brain") in conjunction with the letter נ (numerical value 50), indicating that a restful mind is the root of the Fifty Gates of Understanding.

Brith Milah - Circucism and the Sabbath

Both the Brit Milah and the Shabbath is a sign of *the unique status of the Jewish People. This is reflected* in the fact that the numerical value of Brith HaMilah, ברית מילה "the Covenant of Circumcision" is the same as that of Shhabbath (nav) - 702.

The special powers of the Shabbath are alluded to through the code-language of letter-skips in the passage "And the heavens and the earth were completed..." by the fact that the word ברית (covenant) brith appears at intervals of thirteen in the Torah. These special powers of the Shabbath are wonderfully described in the commentary Ma'or Einayim to Parashat Emor, where the Torah gives some of the laws of the Shabbath and the festivals.

Ma'or Einayim quotes the verse in Ecclesiastes (11:2): "Give a portion to seven, and also to eight." "Seven" refers to the Sabbath, which is observed on the seventh day, and "eight" refers to Brit Milah, which is observed on the eighth day.

Ma'or Einayim writes that in the Musaf (Additional Prayer) on the Sabbath, when the congregation recites the Kedushah, the passage beginning: "A crown is given to You..." all the souls of the Jewish People, even those who are on the lowest level, receive an elevation, by being connected with and Included in the souls of the righteous above, as in the beginning of creation, before the first sin.

The connection between the Sabbath and the spiritual level known as Kedem, the level on which Adam existed before the sin, is revealed by the fact that the word Kedem (b1p) is encoded in our passage at intervals of 43 (see p. 218).

The number 43 is the numerical value of the phrase, 1-1-7-), "the goodness of G-d." The sum of the digits of 43 is 4+3=7, which represents the Sabbath, the Seventh Day.

Whenever we multiply a number by ten, the result expresses the perfection of the original number. When we multiply 43 by ten, the result is 430, which is the numerical value of vs (nefesh, "soul").

The root meaning of the word nefesh is "will" or "desire." This concept of the soul, whose essence is will and desire, finds expression on the Sabbath, the day on which the Torah says that G-d "Ceased [creating] and rested" (וינפשExodus 31:17).

The word for "rested" in this verse,וינפש which is based on the word ("soul").

The digits of 43 are 4 and 3. The number 4 corresponds to the letter ד) 7+ while 3 corresponds to ג Thus 43, 4-3 corresponds to 1-4. When manifested in full perfection, on the Holy Sabbath, 43 becomes 430, nefesh, the desire and will be inherent in 4-3 ,ג-ד. These two letters together spell דג (dag), which means "fish."

Besides being the numerical value of דג (dag, "fish), seven is the gematria ketanah of number of other words connected with the Shabbath meals:

(נר)), "candle" - 250; 2+5+0=7 (יין), "wine" - 70;7+0=7

(חלה))(chalah), "bread" - 43; 4+3=7

Thus (בשר), "meat" - 502; 5+0+2=7

The names of the letters of a ((דג, "fish") are dalet, gimmel.

The word dalet (דלת) contains the word dal (דל), meaning "poor," while gimmel (ג) has the same root as gomel (גומל)), meaning "bestower."

Thus these letters allude to the concept of the poor person who seeks someone who will bestow abundance upon him.

In this light the author of Ma'or Einayim (to Parashat Vayetze) writes that on the Shabbath the Jewish People should feel like poor people yearning for the Bestower, the Holy One, blessed is He to grant abundance to them.

This, explains Ma'or Einayim, is the reason why there is a custom to eat fish on the Shabbath, as we see from the Talmud (Shabbat 119a) which relates the story of Rabbi Yosef Mokir Sabbath, who spent a large sum of money to buy a very expensive fish in order to honor the Sabbath.

The deep meaning of this custom of eating fish on the Shabbath is explained by Ma'or Einayim: On (the first] Shabbath, all the souls' of mankind] were included on the highest level in Adam. Likewise [in subsequent generations] the souls of the Jewish People] are included on the highest level with the souls of the Tzaddikim (the righteous) in the sanctity of (the Sefira off Keter (Crown), as a "memorial of the work of Creation" (זכר למעשה בראשית).

Hence (the Jewish person, on the Sabbath] must include himself with the Tzaddikim, as in the case of Adam.

The elevation of the souls] occurred by means of inclusion. For if a person is separated from the Tzaddik. how can he elevate him? And this is the secret of the phrase in the Musaf Prayer, "...a memorial of the work of Creation."

Thus as the fish, דג)), symbolizes the Jew, who regards himself as spiritually "poor" (דל), and his (ג) from the upper worlds.

From this aspect, the word שבת -Shabbath, " can be analyzed asשב ת– , where the first part, שב(means "he returns,") while the second part the letter ת , being the final letter of the Hebrew alphabet, symbolizes the World To Come.

On the Shabbath the Jewish person subsumes himself within his primordial source. He "returns" (שב) to the aspect of the World To Come (ת) which was available to Adam at the time of Creation.

The special power of the Shabbath, the Seventh Day, is alluded to by the verse in Ecclesiastes (11:2): "Give a portion to seven."

The number seven, made up of four (ד) and three (ג), is the foundation of the Shabbath, the Seventh Day - to yearn for the Sabbath as a fish (דג) yearns for water.

This yearning is expressed by the Jewish People in Lecha Dodi, the song of receiving the Shabbath, in the refrain: "Go forth, my Beloved, towards the bride, let us welcome the Shabbath."

In Hebrew this refrain is structured as a phrase of four words followed by one of three words:

לכה דודי לקראת כלה פני שבת נקבלה.

This is the structure of לכה דודי לקראת כלה the yearning of the poor person (ד) for the Bestower (ג) who grants abundance.

This seven-word refrain consists of twenty-six letters, the numerical value of the name of G-d- י-ה-ו-ה.

A similar structure is found in Kad

' Here too we find seven words, a phrase of four followed by a phrase of three. "שמור וזכור בדבור אחד השמיענו א-ל המיוחד"

This same pattern is also found in the verse recited before the public reading of the Torah in the synagogue:

"And you who are attached to the Lord your G-d - all 'of you are alive today" "ואתם הדבקים בה' אל-ה יכם חיים כלכם היום" (Deuteronomy 4:4).

On a lighter note it is interesting that the wordדגדג, (digdeg,)"he tickled," which denotes another kind of arousal, is a double form of the דג .

The verse in Ecclesiastes quoted above,"Give a portion to seven," continues: "and also to eight."

This alludes to the Brit Milah, the Covenant of Circumcision, which is performed on the eighth day.

By juxtaposing the "seven" and the "eight," the verse hints that the Shabbath and Brit Milah, have something in common - namely, the special power to elevate the Jew to the level of כתר (Crown), the highest sphere in the tree of life.

The connection between the ברית מילה which is performed on the eighth day and the sphere כתר (Crown) is revealed in the numerical value of these two words.

The numerical value of Covenant (ברית) is 612. When we add 8 for the eight days, the total is 620, which is the numerical value of כתר (crown).

QUEEN SABBATH AND THE SPHERE OF KINGSHIP

Queen Sabbath שבת המלכה is related to the sphere of Malchut (Kingship), the seventh of the lower seven sphere). "

" Three days before the Shabbath, the Shabbath emerges from its majestic abode." During these three days a person purifies himself to merit the divine illumination of the three Patriarchs, the illuminations embodied in the three branches of the ש above.

These three days provide a preparation period for the three parts of the soul called Nefesh, Ruach and Neshamah.

The Nefesh resides in the liver, the Ruach in the heart, and the Neshamah in the brain.

Taking the initial letters of the Hebrew names for "liver" (kaved, כבד‎), "heart" (לב, 32) and "brain"מח (mo'ach,) produces the word כלם (kelim, h"vessels"), revealing that the three different parts of the soul are the vessels intended to contain the holiness of the Sabbath.

The heavens, the earth, and all their hosts represent in this world the three divisions of the soul.

Thus we can understand the words of the Kabbalah which say that the universe is likened to a huge man, and man is like a miniature universe. About the verse (Genesis 2:1), "And the heavens and the earth were completed, and all their legions," the commentators state that the word in verse "Vayechulu" ויכלו-‎ "And...were completed" is from the term כלם ("vessels"), and indicates that the heavens and the earth were made to be vessels for receiving the sanctity of the Shabbath.

Thus. the task of man is to prepare in himself the vessels that will receive this sanctity of the Shabbath

The pursuit of the holy seventh attribute of Malchut- Kingship.

THE SANCTITY OF THE SABBATH IN THE PHISICAL WORLD

5 + 2 = 7 250 = נר (candle)

7 + 0 = 7 70 = יין (wine)

7 = דג (fish)

4 + 3 = 7 43 = חלה (bread)

5 + 2 = 7 502 = בשר (meat)

On the Shabbath, the sanctity of Shabbath is stored even in the physical world, so that in using these physical items that are especially for Shabbath, a person elevates that part of him which is physical. With the powerful boost to the spirit which speech provides, he who sanctifies Shabbath by speaking words of Torah has his thought process sanctified through contemplation of holy matters. Contemplation speech and action are the principal components of man, as shown by the name אדם (man).

The letter א. symbolizes the mind and thought process, א, coming from the word אלף which means teaching, wisdom.

The letters ד and the letter , ם are the initial letters of the words דבור (speech) and מעשה (action).

The three branches of the letter ש, symbolize these powers.

The letter formed by the right branch is the letter of wisdom, the letter י, formed by the middle branch is the letter ו of spirit, which is revealed through the power of speech, and the letter ז formed by the left branch symbolizes action.

The whole of man's being is clothed in the holiness of the Shabbath.

אדם in minor numerology equals 9 (1 + 4 + 4 = 9), just as the minor numerology of שבת equals 9 (3 + 2 + 4 = 9), to show us that each one is complemented and completed by the other and that they are tightly bound.

The thought, speech, and action of a man are elevated in different ways.

His thoughts are elevated by being occupied with Torah, which is chiefly thought oriented. His speech and heart are elevated through prayer.

In the world of physical action also the sanctity of the Sabbath is stored, and through his own actions a person can elevate his conduct.

With the powerful boost to the spirit which speech provides, he who sanctifies the Sabbath by speaking words of Torah has his thought process sanctified through contemplation of holy matters.

THOUGHT SPEECH ON THE SABBATH

Thought speech, and action are the principal components of man, as shown by the word אדם (Adam, "man").

The letter א symbolizes thought, since the name of this letter is אלף (alef), a root meaning to learn or teach.

The remaining letters of אדם, i.e. the letter ד and the letter מ are the initial letters of the words דבור (dibur, "speech") and מעשה (ma'aseh, "action").

The three branches of the letter ש, symbolizes these three powers.

The letter י which forms the right branch is the letter of wisdom or thought; the letter ו which forms the middle branch is the letter of spirit, revealed through the power of speech; and the letter ז which forms the left branch symbolizes action.

The body and soul are elevated through the enjoyment of the shabbath with its food and happiness.

The pleasure derived from Shabbath, which symbolizes the abundance of Eden flowing to the garden (גן), can be seen in the letters of the word שבת.

The garden indicates to the attribute of dominion-Kingship, the attribute of the Community of Israel.

בת (daughter), according to mystical sources, also indicates to the attribute of kingship-dominion.

The letter ש symbolizes wisdom, understanding, and knowledge in the upper worlds in the following way:

The letter י of the ש, stands for wisdom, the letter , ז for understanding, and the ו for knowledge.

Therefore, from the word שבת being a construction of ש and בת, we see that wisdom, understanding, and knowledge radiate from the Eden of the upper world to endow the world with the attributed by בת- גן and מלכות .

As we saw before, one of the most important kind of food eaten on shabbath meals, whose the number is seven, is the Fish דג. which. Many reasons are given to this custom, one of them is indicted in the letters דג.

THE SECRET BEHIND דג ON THE SABBATH

The names of the letter of the word דג (Fish) have meaning. The letter ד, דלת as in it the word דל, meaning poor, while the letter ג in דג, the letter name –גימל-Gimel,- has the same root as -bestowed -גומל.

Thus, these letters allude to the concept of the poor person who seeks someone who will bestow abundance upon him .

In this light the author of the book Maor Einaym (to portion Vaigash), writes that on the shabbath, the Jewish person should feel like poor people yearning for the Bestower, the Holy One blessed is He, to grant abundance to them.

This explains, says Maor Einaim is the reason why there is a custom to eat fish on the shabbath, as we see from the Talmud, Shabbat(119a) which states the story of Rabbi Yosef Mokir Shabbath, who spent a large sum of money, to buy a very expensive fish, in order to honor the shabbath.

After long explanation to it, comes out that the fish דג symbolizes the Jew, who regards himself as spiritually poor, and his yearning to be included in the outpouring of abundanceג)),) from the upper world.

This is like the fish in the water open his mouth to have water, so the Jew on the shabbath should drink more a more Torah which compared to water.

The special power of the shabbath the seven day is alluded to by the verse in Ecclesiastes (11:2) "Give a portion to seven".

The number seven made up of four (ד and three (ג), is the foundation of the s

Shabbath, the seventh day- to yearn for the shabbath as a fish yearn for water.

THE STRUCTURE OF THE SIX STANZAS IN THE POEM LECHA DODI

This yearning is express by the Jewish people in the - לכה דודי Lecha Dodi, the song of receiving the shabbath. in the refrain "Go forth my beloved to the bride, let us welcome the Sabbath".

In Hebrew this refrain is structure as phrase of four words followed by three words פני שבת נקבלה .

This is the structure of the word דג the fish ,the yearning of the poor person (ד)) for the Bestower (ג) Who grants abundance.

Additional stanzas of the song Lecha Dodi follow the four –three patterns, representing the recipient who aspires to receive from the bestower.

For example"שמור וזכור בדבור אחד ,"השמיענו א-ל המיוחד"' -Guard and remember in the same utterance – the one GOD told us", GOD is one, and His name is one- for fame and glory and praise" ה' אחד" ושמו אחד לשם ולתפארת ולתהילה."All these stanzas are structured in the pattern of four- three, express ing the yearning of the bride, for the bride groom-until we arrive to the stanza ,"From the beginning from before,[The shabbath] was poured forth,-last in deed but first in thought,"מראש מקדם נסוכה סוף מעשה במחשבה תחילה". Here we find the pattern of three – four, symbolizing the bestower (3) who pours out abundance upon the recipient (4) It is interesting to note that preceding the six stanzas in the pattern of four – three (They are 1-2: the refrain, recited twice, "Go forth, my beloved, towards the bride- let us welcome the Sabbath"'לכה דודי לקראת כלה –פני שבת נקבלה" 3:Guard and remember in the same utterance-the One GOD told us",4 זכור ושמור בדבור אחד השמיענו א-ל המיוחד " : GOD is one and His name is one for fame and glory and praise". "ה' אחד ושמו אחד,לשם ולתפארת ולתהילה".

5: the refrain recited again "Go forth my beloved...

6: "Let us go to greet the shabbats-for it is the source of the blessing" "לקראת שבת לכו ונלכה כי היא מקור הברכה" .

This six stanzas built on the four thee pattern representing the recipient who aspires to receive from the bestower, correspond to the six days of the week, during which the Jewish soul look forward for the shabbath.

Then comes the seven stanza,"From the beginning from before[the Shabbath] was poured –last in deed, but first in thought", corresponding to the seventh day, which pours out its abundance upon the Jewish people.

This seventh word refrain consist of twenty-six letters, the numerical value of the name of GOD - י-ה-ו-ה.

A similar concept is found in the six chapters of Psalms (beginning "Come let us exult"לכו נרננה .which are recited on Friday evening, for Kabalat Shabbah, the service of receiving the Shabbath.

These six psalms correspond to the six days of the week. Then. after the songs " Please with strength "אנא בכח , and "Go fourth my beloved",לכה דודי,come two psalms ,corresponding to the shabbath.

Incidentally, the total number of all eight psalms is 702, which is the numerical value of the word שבת (Rabbi Yakov orbach).

STRUCTURE OF VERSES WITH NUMBERS THREE AND FOUR

On the shabbath the Jewish person finds revealed within himself, a desire, yearning and spiritual longing for GOD, blessed be He, the bestower-a yearning which is expressed in sentences structured on the pattern of four – three.

A similar concept is found in the verse (Deuteronomy, 4:4)"And you who are cleaving to the Lord ,your GOD-all of you are alive today", "ואתם הדבקים בה' א-להיכם-חיים כלכם היום".

This cleaving on the part of the Jewish people causes them to merit an outpouring of divine abundance, from the bestower, symbolized by the pattern of four- threes in psalm (45;6)"פותח את ידך-ומשביע לכל חי רצון", "You open your hand – and satisfy, every being".

Another instance of seven words in the four three pattern, is found in the verse about the Temple offering of the Shabbath for through this offering abundance and blessings come down to the Jewish people.

For example, we find (Numbers 28:9)"And on the shabbath Day, two lambs two lambs- of the first year"וביום השבת שני כבשים-בני שנה תמימים", "And two measures of flour as a meal offering-mixed with oil, and its libation"ושני עשרונים סלת מנחה – בלולה בשמן ונסכו.

In these sentences the four –three patterns symbolizes the yearning and hope of the person who bring the offerings.

On the other hand ,in the sentence (ibid,v.10):"A burnt –offering for the shabbath on its shabbath-in addition to the Continual burnt offering an it libation" ,"עלת שבת בשבתו – על עלת התמיד ונסכה"we find the three – four pattering, alluding to the outpouring abundance from above on the shabbath".

The number of letters in this latter verse is is twenty six ,which is the numerical value of the name of GOD,-י-ה-ו-ה ,

The same number as in the verse "It (Exodus:31:17) is a sign forever, between Me and the children of Israel" "‏,"ביני ובין בני ישראל‏ "אות חיא לעלם‏" and in the refrain "Go fourth my beloved, towards the bride, let us welcome the shabath."‏לכה דודי לקראת כלה,פני שבת נקבלה‏".

The three seven —word verses just quoted regarding the Temple offerings of the shabbath, are parallel to three seven-word sentences, in the passage, "And the heaven and the earth were completed...."

"And on the seventh day, GOD completed His work which He has done "‏ויכל א-להים ביום השביעי מלאכתו אשר עשה‏"

(Genesis, 2:2)

And he rested on the seventh day from all His work which He has done",‏וישבת ביום השביעי מכל מלאכתו אשר עשה‏" And God blessed the seventh Day and sanctified it "‏ויברך א-להים את יום השביעי ויקדש אותו‏"

A similar structure is found in kadish, in the responsive phrase:"‏יהא שמיה רבא מברך לעלם ולעלמי עלמיא‏" , "May his great name will be blessed, forever and ever", which expresses the yearning of the Jewish people for their Father in Heaven.

Here to we find seven words, a phrase of four followed by phrases of three..

This same phrase, is also found in the verse recited before the public reading of the Torah in the synagogue, "And you, who are attached to the Lord your GOG are alive today "‏ואתם הדבקים בה' א-להיכם חיים כלכם היום‏"".

The verse in Ecclesiastes quoted above, "Give portion to seven", continues " and also to eight ."This is the ‏ברית מילה‏ Covenant of circumcision , which is perfumed on the eighth day.

By juxtaposing the seven and the eighth, the verse hints that the shabbath and the ‏ברית מילה‏, circumfusion, have something in common namely, the specialpower to elevate the Jew to the level of the sphere of Crown- ‏כתר‏, which the Shabbath and circumcision connected, as we saw before.

THE CONNECTION OF ברית COVENANT AND THE SABBATH

The connection between the word ברית,(covenant), which is performed on the eighth day, and the crown, is revealed in the numerical value of these two words. The numerical value of ברית is 612 .

When we add 8 for eight days, is 620, the numerical value of the word crown-.כתר

THE SABBATH AND FAITH

The Shabbath, as we said before, strengthens belief that there is a Creator of the world and that He guides His world every day, continuously.

We noted above that the numerical value of שבת ("Shabbath"), 702 is equal to the combined numerical value of two names of G-d, (י-ה-ו-ה-)26) and (אדנ-י)65) plus the numerical value of the word תורה(Torah,611).

The name י-ה-ו-ה alludes to G-d's attribute of Chessed (Kindness), while the name אדנ-י is the name of Din (Strict Justice).

Complete faith is the cognizance that Strict Justice and Kindness are interwoven, complementing, and fulfilling one another.

Faith includes the awareness that we will reach this level too in the future, and then we shall recite a blessing over the evil just as over the good, for all will realize that the kindness of G-d is hidden within seemingly harsh judgments and evil events.

The name -י-ה-ו-ה has the numerical value 26, while אדנ-י has the numerical value 65. Together these names equal 91, the numerical value of אמן (Amen), which is the root of אמונה (emunah, "faith"). On the Sabbath these two names of Kindness and Strict Justice unite.

When we write these two names of G-d one over the other and multiply the numerical value of the first letter of one to ישר (yosher, straightness of heart) and afterwards to complete happiness.

THE SABBATH AND THE NUMBER SEVEN

The Shabbath, like song, is built upon seven basic elements which combine with each other and fulfill one another within the quality of Malchut (Kingship), the seventh sefirah.

The identification of שבת (Shabbat, "Sabbath") with שבע (sheva,"seven") can be seen in the letters שב which begin both words.

The two remaining letters are the ת of and the ע of שבע. The relationship of ת to ע can be understood when we consider that the name of the letter ע is עין (ayin), which means "eye."

Thus the letter ע represents the root of תאוה (ta'awah, "lust") which is symbolized by the letter ת, for people only covet what their eyes see.

The eye as the root of lust is expressed by the fact that the letters of עין (ayin, "eye") precede those of כסף, a root denoting desire.

ע precedes פ

י precedes כ

נ precedes ס

The Kabbalah (Zohar Tosefta, part 1, p. 113b) speaks of the 400 worlds of כסוף (kisuf, "yearning").

Four hundred is according to the holy Shelah that through songs of praise we out off the material shells which cover our souls, and then we are reunited with our Creator.

On the Holy Sabbath these songs of praise help the soul to free itself from the chains of the material world and cleave to its Maker.

According to the Kabbalah, the world of song is very high and very near to the world of repentance, since repentance and song are closely related.

What is their relationship? The concept of תשובה (teshuvah, "repentance") in its essence is related to השבת (HaShabbat, "the Sabbath") as we saw earlier.

THE RELATIONSHIP OF SONG AND SABBATH

The relationship of שבת (Shabbat, "Sabbath") to שירה (shirah, "song") can be understood also according to our explanation of the similarity between the letters ש and the letter ר which is before the letter ש in the alphabet.

If we exchange the lettersא of יראה (awe)with the letter ב the ר in יראה for,ש we have the lettersשיבה ,(returning),indicating to us the fear of Shabbath bring to repentance, which is the foundation of the Sabbathהשבת –תשבה,

The root ofשירה (shirah, "song") is שיר(shir). This is similar to שור (shur), a root that denotes seeing. The "Desert of Shur" (Exodus 15:22) where the children of Israel sojourned after crossing the Sea of Reeds, is called Shur because of the heavenly vision which Israel saw there.

Through song the awe in man's heart is strengthened and he recognizes the world as G-d's creation. Song on the Sabbath helps us straighten our hearts and thereby merit fulfilling the verse (Psalms 97:11),

"Light is sown for the righteous and joy for the straight-hearted." The concept of אור(or, "light") is the basis of nor» (ir'ah, "awe". The attainment of אור (or, "light") brings

One who merits the proper enjoyment of the Sabbath also merits the aspect of Redemption in his] soul. And when all Israel keep the Sabbath properly, total light dwellin the habitants.

Sabbath and Redemption

The Midrash tell us that through the merit earned by observing Shabbath, redemption will come.

The connection of redemption to Shabbath. is understood through the writings of the mystical books which explain that there is a similarity between the letters ש and א since each is formed by the union of the three letters ו,י, , and ז. Thus, א and ש represent unity and harmony. Exile is a result of dispute and division.

The element which brings redemption is unity. These concepts are revealed by the word גאולה (redemption) which is comprised of גל (revelation) and א. Redemption relies on unity.

At the same time, unity relies on the strengthening of the spiritual foundation of man, and this is expressed by the letters which join to form the א and ש, the letters of wisdom, understanding, and knowledge, as described above.

Conflict and quarreling have their foundation in the material world, but in the deep recesses of the soul there is no place for division and strife, for the root of all Jewish souls is one.

The war initiated by Amalek against Jews ,is the root of all the wars of the nations against Israel. What protects the Jewish people from the attack of Amalek? The answer is that the Sabbath day, the Shabbath Day will protect them.

This is reflected by the numerical value of the words יום השבת of the words מלחמת עמלק- -The war of Amalek, the Shabbath Day which equals the numerical value 758.

More ever the number value 758, is the numerical value of the words ברית עולם (eternal covenant) 758, between GOD and the Jewish people, a covenant which find its most perfect expression on the Shabbath day (758).

THE POWER OF THE HOLINESS OF SABBATH TO OVER COME THE EVIL FORCES

The power of the Holiness of the Shabbath to overcome the evil forces of Amalek, is indicated in the commandment to remember the Shabbath and to remember what Amalek did to Jews ,use the word same word זכור "Remember" which appears in the two commandments of remembering.

Interesting numerical value, shows that desecrating of the Shabbath by Jews, delays the coming of the Messiah ,the numerical value of the words desecrating the Shabbath חלול שבת equals 776 coming of Messiah ביאת המשיח equals 776, this against this.

One, who merits the proper enjoyment of Shabbath, also merits the aspect of redemption in his soul, and when all of Israel will keep Shabbath properly, total redemption for all will come.

Israel is the counterpart of Shabbath and through them the world receives the holiness of Shabbath.

The relationship between Israel and the holiness of Shabbath is revealed by the letters "ישראל" (Israel) which are the same as those in לי ראש (for me, the beginning). The origin of Israel is the beginning and highest level. This level is the source ofשבת whose letters follow ראש (top, beginning) in the alphabet, since, as explained above, "from the very beginning it was ordained."

When the soul looks forwards to the Shabbath to disconnect herself from the slavery of the material desires, and yearning for the holiness of the Shbbath, according to kabbalah it brings abundance to the world.

This idea is expressed by two Hebrew words שפע (abundance) and שבע (seven),the number associated with the שבת-Shabbath. The letters

ב and פ in the words שבע and שפע, are letters formed by expelling air from closed lips connected to sphere of מלכות- -kingdom.

There are five groups of letters against the five spheres. So now when we take the word שבע the number associated with the Shabbath ,and exchange the letter ב for the later פ, the result שפע (abundance)

o the throat: א (alef) ח (chet) ה (hei) ע (ayin)
o the palate: ג (gimel) י (yud) כ (kaf) ק (kuf)
o the tongue: ז (zayin) ש (shin) ס (samech) ר (raish) צ (tzadik)
o the teeth: ד (dalet) ט (tet) ל (lamed) נ (noon) ת (tav)

o the lips: ב (bet) ו (vav) מ (mem) פ (pai)

₀SABBATH AND SONG

A special importance is attached to the songs of praise sung on the Shabbath.

This is shown by the significance of the word זמר (song of praise). זמר, can also mean the action of cutting or severing, teaching us, according to the holy Shelah. that through sounds of praise we cut off the material shells which cover our souls, and we are reunited with our Creator.

On the sacred Shabbath these songs of praise help the soul to free itself from the materialistic chains and cleave to its Maker.

According to our mystical tradition the world of song is very high and very near to the world of repentance since repentance and song are closely related.

What is their relationship? תשובה(repentance) in its essence is related to השבת(the Shabbath), as we saw earlier. The relationship of שבת to שירה (singing) will be understood also according to our explanation of the similarity between the letters ש andא. .

Thus שירה is equal toיראה , which is the foundation of Shabbath, as we saw above.

The word שירה is similar to שור (sight). The מדבר שור(desert of Shur), where the Children of Israel went after their exit from the Red Sea, is called so, because of the heavenly vision which Israel saw there, through song.

The fear in man's heart is strengthened, and the perception of the world as a creation of God is recognized. Song (שיר) on the Shabbath helps man to straighten (. (ישר is heart and thereby to merit what is written in the quotation, "Light is sown for the righteous, and joy for the straight of heart." light) is the basis ofיראה (fear). אור brings one to ישר (straightness) of heart and afterward to complete happiness.

As we saw before, the main virtue of man on the Shbbath, is - יראה awe, which brings him to תשובה –Repentance.

This idea is seen in the similarity of the ירא awe, abd שיבה- returning.

If we exchange the lettersא of ירא (awe) with the letter ב and the letter ר with letter ש, letters which follow each other in the order of the alphabet we have the lettersשיבה of the word (returning), indicating to us that the fear of the Shabbath brings to repentance, which is the foundation of the Sabbathתשבה – השבת as the תשבה --Repentance and השבת – the Shabbath, teach us.

The root of word שירה (shirah, "song) שיר (shir), is similar to שור (shur), a root that denotes seeing, as we find in the Torah the words "Desert of Shur" מדבר שור(Exodus 15:22) where the children of Israel sojourned after crossing the Sea of Reeds, is called Shur, שור-because of the heavenly vision which Israel saw there.

Through song the awe in man's heart is strengthened and he recognizes the world as G-d's creation. Song on the Shabbath helps us straighten our hearts and thereby merit to fulfill the verse (Psalms 97:11):

"Light is sown for the righteous and joy for the straight-hearted." The concept of אור (or, "light") is the basis of ירא (ir'ah, "awe". "אור "זרוע לצדיק ולישרי לב שמחה.

The attainment of אור (or, "light") brings one who merits the proper enjoyment of the Shabbath also merits the aspect of Redemption in his soul. And when all Israel keep the Sabbath properly, total light dwells in their habitants.

THE LIGHT OF THE SABBATH

The light that comes to the Jewish homes on the Shabbath, is reflected in the letters of the word שבת.which can be analyzed to the letters ש-בת.

The letter ש according to the book of creation, symbolizes the fire the source of light. On the Shabbath, as the holy Zoar states, "Light- ש, comes to the בת ישראל -daughter of Israel.

The connection of אור light, to the שבת , is indicated in the same numbers of the numerical value of the word 702 , שבת - and the numerical value of the word 207- אור.

Interesting to note that according to Rabbi Kabbalist, Rabbi Isaac Luria, the shape of the three branches of the letter ש ,in the Torah scroll of are the letters ז י ו , forming the letters of the Hebrew word זיו , meaning splendor, which indicates also to the sphere of the Shabbath תפארת- splendor.

THE SABBATH AND THE SPHERE OF LOVING KINDNESS

The Shabath is connected with sphere of חסד - loving kindness, as is indicated in the numbers of the numerical value of the words שבת and חסד Shabbath 702- שבת , which have the same basic digits as 72 , the numerical value of the word - חסדloving kindness.

Likewise, the Shabbath is connected with the sphere of מלכות Kingship whose root is the name of GOD י-ה-ו-ה ,which connotes the attribute of תפארת (splendor)and Mercy.

The name of GOD י-ה-ו-ה,the name of Loving kindness, is alluded to in the initial letters of the verse "Six days And the heavens were completed"י, "יום השישי ויכלו השמים".

As we saw before, on the- שבת Shabbath, the attributes of loving kindness and kingship prevails.

This is revealed through the divine names,31) א-ל) the name of GOD representing Kindness and the name of GOD,65), אדנ-י) representing Kingship.

This is hinted in the final letters of those same four words יום השישי ויכלו השמים.The letters,מ-ו-י-ם,whose numerical value is 96, equals to the names of GOD , -31) א-ל)–loving Kindness ,and the name 65)אדנ-י)-Kingship is the basis of the existence of the world.

NAMES OF GOD RESCUE JEWS FROM POWERS OF EVIL

These names of GOD rescue the Jewish People, from the forces of Evil, whose prime angle is called סם, whose numerical value is 100, and his mate, the negative force known as the Lilith, whose numerical value is 480.

The latter two have the combine numerical value 580, which equals the numerical value of the name שעיר, the land of Esau, and the numerical value of the words גיא צלמות, "The valley of shadow of death".

Through observing the Shabbath, the Jewish People merit the sanctity, of those divines God's names.

The three names, אדנ-י, -ה-ו-ה-י, א-ל, which have the numerical value 122. With the addition of the number the number of the two evil forces, we get the number 702, the same numerical value as שבת-Shabbath.

This indicates that these evil forces should be subdued by the power of the holiness of Shabbath as , stated by the Holy Zohar, and as is mention by the Kabbalist, Rabbi Isaac Luriay in his song on the the third meal of the Shabbath בני היכלא,. the sentence,"To annul all the evil forces".

Rabbi Isaac Luria, further explains the connection between the divine name of GOD א-ל.

The name of Loving Kindness, connected with the Shabbath, whose numerical value is thirty-one. and the sanctity of the Shabbath in the book (Pri Etz Chaim, Hashabbat ch,24),he states that this name of GOD corresponds to the thirty one hours, during which the Shabbath prevail .

Six hours from noon Friday, until nightfall, twenty four hours of the Shabbath itself, and one hour in the night when the Shabbath departs from us .

These thirty-one hours of the sanctity of Shabbath, says Rabbi Isaac Luria, correspond to the thirty one kings, represent 31 roots of the negative spiritual forces whom Joshua concurred, when the Jewish people entered the land of Israel (Joshua,12-24).

Rabbi Isaac Luria concludes, "This matter is alluded to by the phrase in the prayer, "GOD the King, who sits on the throne of Mercy...א-ל מלך יושב על כסא רחמים,".

The Seeds of Humility, Faith, and Peace

Shabbath, like song, is built upon seven basic elements which combine with each other and fulfill one another within the מלכות (dominion). The identification of שבת with שבע (seven) can be seen in the letters שב, which are the first letters of both words.

The relationship of the letter ת to the letter ע can be understood by the element of עין (eye) which is what the letter y represents.

In this respect, the ע symbolizes the root of men (lust) which is symbolized by the letter ת, for no man covets anything except that which his eyes see.

The eye as the root of lust is expressed by the fact that the letters of עין (eye) precede the letters of the word כסף (money), which comes from the term כסופים (yearnings, desires).

The mystical texts mention 400 worlds of yearning and desire; 400 is the numerical value of the letter ת.

NAMES OF GOD י-ה-ו-ה- (sphere of Mercy)AND THE NAME אדנ-י NAME OF KINGSHIP ON SABBATH

The pursuit of the holy seventh attribute of מלכות (dominion) is depicted by the fact that mastery over the powers of one's soul is attained through a disconnecting (שב) of the power of the covetous eye (ע). Similarly, the attainment of holiness on Shabbath requires the severance (שב) of the power of lust (ת).

Shabbath, as we said before, plants in a man's heart the belief in a Creator of the world who guides His world every day, continuously. We noted that the numerical value of שבת is equal to that of "תורה + אדנ-י" + -י-ו-ה- ה.

The name of God -י-ה-ו-ה is the name of loving-kindness while the name of God- אד-ני is the name of judgment. Complete faith is the cognizance faith that judgment and mercy are interwoven, complementing, and fulfilling one another.

Ultimately, our sages tell us, mankind will reach this awareness: "In the ultimate future, even over troubles they will bless the Almighty with the blessing הטוב והמטיב " the blessing that is now said only when something good occurs; for they will realize that in judgment and evil, too, the kindness of God is hidden.

The name י-ה-ו-ה adds up to a numerical value of 26 while "אדנ-י" is equal to 65.

Together these names equal 91, the numerical value of אמן (faith). On the Shabbath these two names unite along with judgment and mercy. When we write these two names of God one over the other thus:

י יקוקxו אx נ

ה אדניxה דxי

Multiplying the first letter of one name by the first letter of the other, then the second letter of one na me by the second of the other, etc., the result is 380.

The numerical value of the word שלום (peace), when we add to it the number of its letters, is also 380. The Bnei Yissaschar, states that this comes to teach us the close connection of the attribute of peace with the attributes of judgment and mercy.

THE ATTRIBUTE OF PEACE RESTS ON THE JEW ON THE SABBATH

On the Shabbath the attribute of peace rests on the Community of Israel, as the Shabbath prayer says, "He spreads the shelter of peace over us and over all Israel."

The commands to "remember" and to "observe" the Shabbath, given in a "single utterance," allude to judgment and mercy which unite on Shabbath. "Observe" is the aspect of judgment and "remember" that of mercy. Perfect faith is attained on the holy Shabbath.

The Torah passage beginning: "And the heavens and the earth were completed..." (Genesis 2:1-3), which is the culmination of the account of Creation, contains thirty-five words.

The numerical value of, יהודי a Jew, fits with Midrash that world was created for the Torah, and the Jews who are keeping the Torah.

And there are thirty-five verses in that account (ibid. 1:1-2:3).

The thirty-second verse is: "And the heavens and the earth were completed, and all their legions" (ibid. 2:1). The numerical value, of thirty-two, as represented by Hebrew letters, is 32, which also spells לב ("heart

The thirty-fifth verse, which summarizes the account of Creation, is: "These are the generations of the heavens and the earth when they were created, on the day when G-d made earth and heavens".

THE NUMBER 49-7X7AND THE SABBATH

There are forty-nine letters in this verse which summarizes the account of creation.

The tradition of writing a Torah scroll tells us that in this verse the letter ה numerical value (5) in the word בהבראם (meaning "when they were created") is to be written smaller than the other letters. Not counting this small, ה there are forty-nine letters in this verse.

Forty-nine, being seven times seven, represents.

This same number of letters, forty-nine, appears again in a passage where the Torah commands Sabbath observance as an eternal sign between the Holy One, blessed is He, and the Nation of Israel.

The final forty-nine Hebrew letters of that passage read: "For in six days G-d made the heavens and the earth, and on the seventh day He ceased and rested","וביום השביעי שבת וינפש".

Why is the number of verses in the entire account of Creation (35) equal to the number of letters in the verse describing the first Sabbath, "And the heavens and the earth were completed..?"

This emphasizes the connection between the creation of the universe, and the Shabbath, which our Sages (in the wording of the Shabbath night Kiddush) called: "a commemoration of the act of creation."

THE POEM "LECHA DODI" ON THE EVE OF THE SABBATH

In the poem, Lecha Dodi ,which we sing during Kabalat Sabat ,the welcoming of the Sabbath on Friday just before the evening Prayer.

This poem was written by tho holy Kabbalist, Rabbi Shlomo Hlevi Alkabrtz, the brother in law of the greatKabbalist Rabbi Mosh Cordovero, who lived in Safed.

The poem is based on Tractate Shabat(119a) which relates that Rabbi Chanina was accustomed to enwrapping himself in a special garment on Friday after noon, and say" let us go forth to greet the Shabbath the Queen.

And Rabbi Yanai had a custom toput on special clothes on Friday after noon and say, "Come O Bride, Come O Bride".

This poem has ten parts which indicates to the ten Spheres. One of them which is about the Holy Shabbath."סוף מעשה, מראש מקדם נסוכה, במחשבה תחילה"",as we saw before this comes after six stanzas, which have structure of Four- Three, representing the longing of the children of Israel to cleave to GOD.

The structure of the stanza מקדם מראש , is Three –Four, indicating to the pouring the abundance to the children of Israel.

קדם AND THE SABBATH

The word קדם, meaning "from the beginning, from before (the Shabbath) was poured forth, last in deed, but first in thought".

From here we see that the allusion to קדם is the supernal source of the Shabbath.

In the Hebrew alphabet, the letters of the word ראש -beginning, are those that immediately precede the letters of שבת.

The expression מראש "from the beginning", hints, Look back towards the beginning(of the alphabet. i.e the letters that precede ראש.

These letter spell שבת. The next word is , "from kedem", Thus, the poem reminds us that the shabbas come.קדם

Special importance is given to the connection between Israel and the Shbbath.Bereshit Rabba(11:12)cites Rabbi Shimon bar Yochai(his name שמעון בר יוחי has the numerical value 702 ,which equals that of שבת).

THE PARTNERSHIP BETWEEN ISRAEL AND THE SABBATH

The partnership between Israel and the Shabbath is a pre-condition for the existence of the the universe, as the Talmud reveals in tractate Shabbath,

"Who ever recite Kidush, saying ,"And heaven and earth were completed", it is as if he were a partner with the Holy one, blessed is He, in the creation of the universe, as it is said ויכלו were completed.

Do not read it ויכלו, were completed, but ,they completed. They, GOD and his partner, the children of Israel complete the heaven and the earth.

The Talmud there, goes on to say", From where we learn that saying is like doing, because it said in psalm (33:6) "By the word of GOD, the Heaven were made".

THE POWER OF SPEECH

Speech is the basis of the creation". Therefore, through their speaking of the verse about creation in the Shabbath Kidush, Israel becomes partners in the ongoing work of Creation.

Thus, when they sanctify and observe the Sabbath, they are also maintaining the existence of the universe which GOD created,

The dependence of the universe upon the Holy Shabbath stem from the fact that the Shabbath is the name f the Holy One, blessed is He, as the holy Zohar states (Yitro 88b:"the Shabbath is the name of the Holy One, blessed is He, which is peace in every direction.

Just as the purpose of the special power of the Shabbath is to give form to the weekdays, so too, the purpose and special power of Israel to is give form to humanity.

This is why the passage "And the heaven and earth were completed" is the only where the name of Israel is encoded at intervals of fifty letters.

Fifty, is the numerical value of the letter נ, which represents the soul נשמה, whose foundation is the phrase, שמה-נ(the 50)נ)is there.

The Shabbath is the soul of the nations of the world. The basis of existence of the universe is the letters of the Hebrew alphabet, as we see in the verse (psalm, 33:6):"by the word of GOD the heavens were made".

THE POWER OF THE HEBREW LETTERS

These letters not only were the instrument of Creation, but they have the power to keep the universe in existence, as the Sages of Kabbalah said regarding

the verse: (119:89),"Forever GOD, your word stands in the heaven", i.e. the continued standing of the heavens, depends upon the word of GOD, the word, of course his word, is composed of letters.

These letters derive their power from the divine Name which permeates them. and the Shabbath is the inner essence which gives the letters of the Hebrew alphabet, to sustain the world.

The Shabbath, as the foundation of the word is indicated in the letters of the word שבת,–שת -ב שת,, from the word ב –בית,the house, תשתית- basis. symbolizing the world.

THE BASIS OF THE CREATION THE AWE AND FEAR OF GOD

The awe and fear of the Shabbath is the basis of Creation. As King Salomon says in his book, Ecclesiastes (3:14)"ג" "האלהים עשה שיראו מלפניו".

"GOD MADE THAT THEY will fear Him"

In the end of Ecclesiastes says King Solomon, "The sum of the matter, when all is said and done: "Revere God, and observe His commandments! For this applies to all mankind."

The fact that ירא --Fear is the foundation of creation, is revealed in the word -בריאה, creation, whose letters in different order spell, ביראה meaning for the sake of Fear".

Through reciting the passage "And the heavens and earth were completed....." The Jewish person fulfills the purpose of creation and thereby, becomes a partner with the Holy One, blessed is He, in, maintaining the existence of the universe.

THE SECRET OF THE בראשיתIN THE BEGINNING

Thus the opening word of the Torah, בראשית ,"In the beginning "is compose of the letters שבת – ירא The first part, the word ירא ,is imperative from of -יראה, Fear, one should fear, or alternatively,ירא ,one who fears.

The second part is שבת - Shabbath. That is, the very beginning of Creation account hints that the purpose of Creation is ירא – ,fear of GOD. Fear expressed through observing the Shabbath.

The Malbim explains that the fear is as the world was created in such a way, that any second is a metrical that the world does not collapse, as a result of the orbit of the stars, and other powers which s

It is interesting to note, the because of this, Albert Einstein said that it must must be someone who watches that things like this will not happen.

One of the traditional of discovering hidden allusions in the Torah is to look at the words formed by the initial of final letters. the first words of the Torah,"בראשית ברא א-להים",the final letters of the words, form the word אמת –Truth, one of the three pillars, on which the world stands, as it is brought in the Ethics of the Fathers.

The word אמת, comes out also in Genesis (1:30)in the words "וירא א-להים את ","And GOD saw", the final letters אמת ,Truth.

In the end of the story of the Creation with the Shabbath, the words are (Genesis, 2:3)" ברא א-להים לעשות ", "GOD created to do".

The Talmud (Shabbat, 55, a) states, "The seal of GOD, the signet with which, as it were, He seals his decrees, is אמת -Truth.

And here we see that the signet with
which He sealed the account of the world.

SABBATH IS THE WELLSPRING TO THE WORLD TO COME

The Sabbath, the wellspring of the World to come, is created through the letter n, the letter of the World to Come.

The return of the soul to its source in the World to Come, is revealed through the construction of the word שבת from the שב and the letter ת.

The Holy Shabbath, states Rabbi Tzadock Hakoen (Genesis, Portion Bereshith) contains within it the sanctity of the Sabbatical Year (Sehmita), corresponding to the number seven.

As well as the sanctity of the Jubilee Year (yovel) corresponding to the number fifty.

These numbers Seven and Fifty, are connected to the spheres מלכות –Kingship, (7) and בינה-Understanding (50).

This is what the Holy Zohar (part 2p.42b) states; the Shabbath is connected with spheres of בינה- -Understanding -and מלכות - Kingship.

This connection is manifested in the letters of the word- שבת Shabbath.

SABBATH THE SPERES OF בינה UNDERSTANDING AND מלכות- KINGSHIP

The word שבת can be analyzed as ש-בת. The letter שין, ש is related to the word שינון , which means to repeat and review what one studied.

This is of course the activity which brings a person to בינה –Understanding.

The remaining letters, spell בת -Daughter, one of the names referring to the sphere of מלכות- Kingship (Sfath Emet by the the Rama of Pano).

Thus, the letters -of the word שבת - Shabbath, express the light (ש) of the sphere of kingdom (בת), the Glory of GOD.

The numerical value of the words, the "light of Kingship"- "אור מלכות", equals 703 which equal the numerical value of the word שבת, with the total.

This shows that the Shabbath is a mean to achieve connection with divinity, connected with the sphere of—מלכות kingship.

Joining the the number of -בינה. Understanding -50 and the number 7 מלכות – Kingship, makes the number 57, which is the numerical value of the names of GOD31),-אל) the name of loving kindness, and the name of GOD 26) י-ה-ו-ה), the name of Mercy, which the Jew gets, by observing the Shabbath.

THE SECRET OF THE WORD כל -ALL

The number fifty, is the numerical value of the word All- כל, which is one of the names of the Shabbath, as the Zohar Chadash states, (part 2.p44b):

"The Shabbath is called כל -All, for on the Shabbath a person should see himself as if all his work has been completed".

The prophet Isiah (58; 14) tells us that when we observe the Shabbath we receive "the Inheritance of Jacob".

The level of כל was achieved by our forefather Jacob, as he told Esau (Genesis, 33"11) "I have all (כל).

Every Jewish person can merit to receive כל (All) as our Sages say (tractate Shabat 118 b) "Who ever takes pleasure in the Shabath, his heart's desire is given to him"

תפארת – SPLENDOR THE SPHERE OF SABBATH

According to the Kabbakah (Kehilat Yakovs.v. (שבת the Shabbath is connected to the sphere תפארת (Splendor).

The sphere which Jacod is connected with after Abraham – Loving kindness, Isaac Strength.

Regarding the Shabbath, we see this manifested in the root of the word תפארת.

The root is פאר, the full numerical value of the letters of the word פאר, פא, אלף, ריש, whose numerical value is 702, equals that of שבת-Shabbath- 702.

Interesting to note, that the numbers of the numerical value of the פאר which is 281.are the same as the numerical value of יעקב– Jacob 182.

Similar idea is according to theKabbalah in the name ישראל –Israel א-ל -מימין –שיר-משמאל א-ל, """– the name of loving kindness on the right and שיר- song the left(according to the Kabbalah singing has to do with Strength).

The Shabbath then is a time of unity.as the relationship of the influencer and the recipient - Strength and Loving kindness prevails.

Idea which we saw before in the stances of the poem Lecha Dodi, Four -Three –Three- Four, idea which also is in the ten commandments on the Shabbath זכור-שמור זכור -- Influencer, שמור- Recipient.

The idea that things on Shabbath are double, like the לחם משנה , the two loaves, the double sheep's in the offering of the Shabbath. An extra נשמה- Soul that a Jew gets on the Shabbath.

This idea of the double on the Shabbath is expressed by the double times of the numerical value of the name ישראל-Israel -541, it comes to the number 1082, which is equal to the numerical value of the sphere of the Shabbath-תפארת (splendor) 1081 with total .

Adding the total in this case, indicates that "Israel"come from the sphere of (splendor).

The function of the sphere of תפארת -Splendor is to produce balance and harmony between opposites such as—חסד Loving kindness and גבורה – Strength right and left,

THE FOUNDATION OF ISRAEL

The foundation of Israel is the creative interaction between two Jews, influencer and recipient, right ad left. Hence twice-ישראל – Israel, 1082 as we saw before, is derived from the sphere of תפארת, the spiritual root of the Shabbath.

The numbers 1082 have the same numbers as Jacob 182, 281 פאר, showing the connection of Jacob to the sphere of תפארת (splendor).

According to the book of creation (related to Abraham, our father), there is a connection between the Shabbath and one of the organs of the human face, namely the mouth.

This is why special importance is attributed to our speech on the Shabbath.

Thus the prophet Isiah (58:13) tells us that on the Shabbath we must be careful"not to pursue your every dayneeds, nor speak a word about such pursuits."

The connection between the Shabbath and the mouth can be seen in the symbolism of the seven branched candelabrum (menorah (מנורה) which was one of the main implements in the Tabernacle and the Holy Temple.

THE SYMBOL OF THE MENORAH

The Menora consists of a central branch, from which six branches extend, three on each side.

According to the Midrash Rabbah (Shemot, Truma) the six branches of the Menorah, correspond to the six days of the week, while the central branch corresponds tit e Shbbath.

Alternatively, the seven branches correspond to the seven of the organs in the human face-two eyes, two ears, two nostrils and the mouth.

The central stem correspond to the mouth, The fact that the central stem of the Menorah correspond to the mouth and to the Shabbath shows that these two, the mouth and the Shabbath are connected with each other.

It is interesting to note that the word candelabrum- מנרה when spelled without the letter ו,the names of letters are מם נון ריש הא, equals the numerical value of .702- שבת

The mouth which is the basis of the power of speech is associated, according to the Kabbalah(Khilt Yakov,s.v. (פהwith the sphere מלכות -Kingship, which is associated with the Shabbath ,as we saw before.

The numerical value of the word mouth - פה is 85, which is equal to the numerical value of the מילה—circumcision.

We have seen above the connection between the Shabbath and the Covenant of Circumcision.

THE HUSBAND AND WIFE ON THE SABBATH

We noted before, that the numerical value of the words ברית המילה 702- the covenant of Circumcision equals the numerical value of שבת- 702-the Shabbath.

The two candles we light on the eve on the Shabbath, correspond, according to our Sages, to the two aspects of the Shabbath observance, mention in the ten commandments "זכור""-Remember" and "שמור"-Guard". Remember correspond to the male, the husband

while guard correspond the female, the wife.

The numerical value of the word נר - candle, is 250.

Thus, the two candles total 500 which equals the number of the limbs of man – 248 – and woman – 252, the four additional limbs of the woman, are in the womb.

The number 500 is also the numerical value of the words "פרו ורבו", "be fruitful and multiply" (Genisis, 1:28, 9:11) a primary commandment which performed by man and woman together.

According to the Kabbalah this commandment is especially connected with the Shabbath.

The number 500 is also the numerical value of the full inner letters of the name of GOD connected to the sphere of foundation, שדי שין ד-ש יין,לת,וד, „דלת יוד equals 500.

THE CONNECTION BETWEEN SABBATH AND PEACE

The connection between Shabbath and Peace is revealed by the holy Zohar (part 3, p.176b) cited by Shem Mishmuel to prtion Pinchas, in the book Numbers:

"When the Holy One blessed is He, created the world, he was not capable of existing. He came and caused Peace to rest upon it."

" And what is peace? It is the Shabbath which brings peace above and below".

"Afterwards however impurity increased in the world, and exile spread".

"However, another Shabbath is needed in order that the quality of peace, which is the ultimate completion of the quality of truth should appear".

Truth and peace are interconnected, as it is revealed in the passage "And the heavens and earth were completed..."in which the word - אמת Truth is encoded twice both times in letters skip.

Fourteen is the numerical value of the word – יד-hand. This fits with the verse"אף די יסדה ארץ וימיני טיפחה שמים"

"Even My hand [*yadi*] has laid the foundation of the earth, and My right hand [*vimini*] has spread out the heavens" (<u>Isaiah 48:13</u>).

The connection between the Shabbath and peace is also revealed by the Talmud (shabat 25 b) brings the verse from Lamentations (3:17) "My soul is uncaredred for, without peace".On this the Talmud comments that "peace" means kindling the Shabbath

The candle symbolizes the soul as we find in Proverbs (20:27).

"The soul of man is the candle of GOD"."נשמת אדם," "נר ה' The light of the candle. Symbolizing, the illumination of the soul, brings peace.

This is reflected in the fact that the "inner" numerical value of the full numerical value of the letters of the word הנר – "the candle equals the numerical value of הנר יש ו נ ר י ה-376 -376- שלום -. .

The peace of the Shabbath is the light of the Shabbath which simulates the soul (ben yeohyada, to Shabbath 25b).

The existence of the world depends upon peace which in turn depends upon the Shabbath.

Because of this connection between the Shabbath and peace, the kabbalist Rabbi Chaim Vital (Pri etz Chaim, Shaa Hshabbat, ch 14) instructs us that after the prayer service on Shabbath night "you should go to your home, and say in loud voice "שבת שלום"-Shabbath of peace.

SABBATH DEFENDS ISRAEL FROM THEIR ENEMIES

As it is known, the root of all wars of the nations against Israel were initiated by the evil force of Amalek- עמלק.

What protects the Jewish people fom the attacks of Amalek? The answer is the Shabbath Day.

This reflected by the numerical value of יום השבת -Shabbath Day- 758, which equals the numerical value of the words מלחמת עמלק- The war of Amalek-758.

Moreover, the number 758 is the numerical value of the words ברית עולם –Eternal Covenant-758, for the War of Amalek is directed against the eternal covenant between GOD and Jewish people, a covenant which finds its most perfect expression on the Shabbath Day (758).

SABBATH DAY OF UNITY AND JOY

The Zohar (part3.p 159b) states that the Shabbath Day is the day of "the joining of the Sun and the Moon".

This is an allusion to the joining of the spheres of חכמה-Wisdom symbolized by the Sun, with בינה -Understanding, symbolized by the Moon.

The joining of the sun and the moon also symbolizes the joining of the brain and the heart.

In the Shabbath night Kiddush we recite verses which conclude the account of the creation of heaven and earth.

We begin with the last two words of (Genesis ch.1) and the then continue "And the heaven and the earth were completed", which is the beginning of ch.2.

Thus, the first four Hebrew words recited are "יום הששי ויכלו השמים" –"The six day, And the heaven were created".

Why does the Torah place the allusion to the name of GOD precisely in the verses which conclude the account of the creation and begin the topic of the Shabbath?

The commentary of Baal Haturim explains that this name appears like a signature to the work of the creation. It means that GOD whose signature is truth created the world and sign with is name י-ה-ו-ה.

Thus His signature in the Torah is His signature upon the creation. It informs us that the Holy One bless be He, brought the world into existence and maintains it, as is written(Isaiah 40:26) "Lift your eyes to the heavens and see who created all these"-that is, by looking at Creation itself we recognize that GOD created it.

The initial letters of these words form the name of GOD י-ה-ו-ה. This name is also spelled out by the initial letters of psalm (96:11) "ישמחו השמים ותגל הארץ","The heavens rejoice and the earth exult".

The reason that the name of GOD appears in the End of the Creation says Rabbi Gedaliah Hlevy Shor: "This teaches that the name of GOD is revealed in the world there is joy, and exultation.

The same concept is expressed in the Shabbath Additional -prayer מוסף, ישמחו במלכותך – Those who observe the Shabbath will rejoice in sovereignty.

Even though the commandment of halachic obligation of Joy applies only to the holidays and not to the Shabbath, never the less the joy of the Shaath is a reality stemming from the pleasure f the Day of Rest.

SABBATH THE FOUNDATION THE WORLD

The world exists in the merit of the Shabbath, and all aspects of the Shabbath are double –for example, the two loaves of bread at each meal, the two lambs offered at the Shabbath additional Offering and so on.

This is because the foundation of the Shabbath is זכור - Remember and שמור -Guard.

The term זכור corresponds to the masculine, the influencer, while שמור - Guard corresponds to the feminine.

The existence of the world is based upon the principle of "man and woman "as the Talmud (Bava Batra 74 b) states:

Every thing that the Holy one, blessed be He created in His world ,he created in the form of male and female, as it is said (Isaiah 20:4: " With the divine name י- ה, GOD formed worlds".

The letter י symbolize Man- א י ש, while the letter ה symbolize the woman אשה.

According to the Kabbalah the letter י, the first letter of GOD name י-ה-ו-ה, represent חכמה -Wisdom, which depends on the brain, while the letter ה the second letter of GOD name which depends upon the heart represents Understanding.

These two attributes were the attributes with which GOD created the Worlds, as is written: (Provers: 3:19) "By wisdom GOD laid the earth, and by understanding he set the heavens in place".

For this reason, says the commentator Kli Yakar. GOD signed His creation with his name י-ה which alludes to the influencer, with His the masculine, represented by the letter י , and the recipient, the feminine represented by the letter ה .

This duality is the foundation of everything in the world, for the existence of the world depends upon the interaction between these two forces.

About the Author

Rabbi Glazerson is a respected figure in Jewish spirituality who offers profound guidance on various aspects of Jewish life. His teachings focus on prayer, ethical behavior, and personal growth, emphasizing the importance of connecting with one's inner self and cultivating a strong relationship with God. He is known for his warmth, compassion, and genuine care for others, making Judaism accessible and relevant to people from all walks of life. Through his teachings, Rabbi Glazerson inspires individuals to live meaningful lives filled with love, kindness, and a deep connection to their faith.

Read more at Www.mglazerson.com.